A JOURNEY
OF RICHES

The Way of the Leader

11 Insights Into the New Paradigm of Leadership

Published by Motion Media International
Editors: Vanessa Corr, Gwendolyn Parker, and Chris Drabenstott
Cover Design: Motion Media International
Typesetting & Assembly: Motion Media International
Printing: Amazon and Ingram Sparks

Creator: John Spender - Primary Author
Title: *A Journey Of Riches – The Way of the Leader*
ISBN Digital: 978-1-925919-27-1
ISBN Print: 978-1-925919-28-8
Subjects: Self-Help, Motivation/Inspiration and Leadership.

Acknowledgments

R eading and writing is a gift that very few give to themselves. It is such a powerful way to reflect and gain closure from the past; reading and writing is a therapeutic process. The experience raises one's self-esteem, confidence and awareness of self.

I learned this when I collated the first book in the *A Journey of Riches* series, which now includes twenty-four books with over 250 different co-authors from more than forty different countries. It's not easy to write about your personal experiences, and I honor and respect every one of the authors who have collaborated in the series thus far.

For many of the authors, English is their second language, which is a significant achievement in itself. In creating this anthology of short stories, I have been touched by the amount of generosity, gratitude and shared energy that this experience has given everyone.

The inspiration for *A Journey of Riches, The Way of the Leader* was an inspiration born from the various chats that I had with my fellow co-author Stefan Almér. Initially he was going to collaborate in the book before this one *The Attitude of Gratitude*, Stefan has an extensive leadership background. We were two weeks out from proofreading the previous book and his chapter was finished. However after I told him the theme for the next book and after two days of pondering the idea he withdrew from *The Attitude of Gratitude* book and decided to rework his chapter. My sincere thanks to Stefan for indirectly influencing the theme for this book you are about to read. *Of course*, I could not have created this book without the ten other co-authors who all said

i

YES when I asked them to share their insights and wisdom. Just as each chapter in this book makes for inspiring reading, each story represents one chapter in the life of each of the authors, with the chief aim of having you, the reader, live a more inspired life. Together, we can overcome our fears and live a more fulfilling adventure.

I want to thank all the authors for entrusting me with their unique memories, encounters and wisdom. Thank you for sharing and opening the door to your soul so that others may learn from your experience. I trust the readers will gain confidence from your successes, and also wisdom, from your failures.

I also want to thank my family. I know you are proud of me, seeing how far I have come from that ten-year-old boy who was learning how to read and write at a basic level. Big shout out to my Mom, Robert, Dad, Merril; my brother Adam and his daughter Krystal; my sister Hollie, her partner Brian, my nephew Charlie and niece, Heidi; thank you for your support. Also, kudos to my grandparents, Gran and Pop, who are alive and well, and Ma and Pa, who now rest in peace. They accept me just the way I am with all my travels and adventures around the world.

Thanks to all the team at Motion Media International; you have done an excellent job at editing and collating this book. It was a pleasure working with you on this successful project, and I thank you for your patience in dealing with the various changes and adjustments along the way.

Thank you, the reader, for having the courage to look at your life and how you can improve your future in a fast and rapidly changing world.

Thank you again to my fellow co-authors: Stefan Almér, Kim Wen, Izaak Coetzee, Debi Beebe, Elizabeth Jennifer Chua,

Michelle Gardiner, Lillian Tahuri, Mariese B. Vacalares, Russell Futcher, Ciara McArdle.

We would greatly appreciate an honest review on Amazon if this book inspires you. This is how we gain more readers to find our inspiring book!

With gratitude,
John Spender

Praise For A Journey of Riches Book Series

"The *A Journey of Riches* book series is a great collection of inspiring short stories that will leave you wanting more!"

~ Alex Hoffmann, Network Marketing Guru.

"If you are looking for an inspiring read to get you through any change, this is it!! This book is comprised of many gripping perspectives from a collection of successful international authors with a tone of wisdom to share."

~ Theera Phetmalaigul, Entrepreneur/Investor.

"*A Journey of Riches* is an empowering series that implements two simple words in overcoming life's struggles.

By diving into the meaning of the words "problem" and "challenge," you will find yourself motivated to believe in the triumph of perseverance. With many different authors from all around the world coming together to share various stories of life's trials, you will find yourself drenched in encouragement to push through even the darkest of battles.

The stories are heartfelt personal shares of moving through and transforming challenges into rich life experiences.

The book will move, touch and inspire your spirit to face and overcome any of life's adversities. It is a truly inspirational read. Thank you for being the kind open soul you are, John!!"

~ Casey Plouffe, Seven Figure Network Marketer.

"A must-read for anyone facing major changes or challenges in life right now. This book will give you the courage to move through any struggle with confidence, grace and ease."

~ Jo-Anne Irwin, Transformational Coach and Best Selling Author.

"I have enjoyed the *Journey of Riches* book series. Each person's story is written from the heart, and everyone's journey is different. We all have a story to tell, and John Spender does an amazing job of finding authors and combining their stories into uplifting books."

~ Liz Misner Palmer, Foreign Service Officer.

"A timely read as I'm facing a few challenges right now. I like the various insights from the different authors. This book will inspire you to move through any challenge or change that you are experiencing."

~ David Ostrand, Business Owner.

"I've known John Spender for a while now, and I was blessed with an opportunity to be in book four in the series. I know that you will enjoy this new journey, like the rest of the books in the series. The collection of stories will assist you with making changes, dealing with challenges and seeing that transformation is possible for your life."

~ Charlie O' Shea, Entrepreneur.

"*A Journey of Riches* series will draw you in and help you dig deep into your soul. These authors have unbelievable life stories of purpose inside of them. John Spender is dedicated to bringing peace, love and adventure to the world of his readers! Dive into this series, and you will be transformed!"

~ Jeana Matichak, Author of *Finding Peace*.

"Awesome! Truly inspirational! It is amazing what the human spirit can achieve and overcome! Highly recommended!!"

~ Fabrice Beliard, Australian Business Coach and Best Selling Author.

"*A Journey of Riches* Series is a must-read. It is an empowering collection of inspirational and moving stories, full of courage, strength and heart. Bringing peace and awareness to those lucky enough to read to assist and inspire them on their life journey."

~ Gemma Castiglia, Avalon Healing, Best Selling Author.

"The *A Journey of Riches* book series is an inspirational collection of books that will empower you to take on any challenge or change in life."

~ Kay Newton, Midlife Stress Buster, and Best Selling Author.

"*A Journey of Riches* book series is an inspiring collection of stories, sharing many different ideas and perspectives on how to overcome challenges, deal with change and to make empowering choices in your life. Open the book anywhere and let your mood choose where you need to read. Buy one of the books today; you'll be glad that you did!"

~ Trish Rock, Modern Day Intuitive, Best Selling Author, Speaker, Psychic & Holistic Coach.

"*A Journey of Riches* is another inspiring read. The authors are from all over the world, and each has a unique perspective to share that will have you thinking differently about your current circumstances in life. An insightful read!"

~ Alexandria Calamel, Success Coach and Best Selling Author.

"The *A Journey of Riches* book series is a collection of real-life stories, which are truly inspiring and give you the confidence that no matter what you are dealing with in your life, there is a light at the end of the tunnel, and a very bright one at that. Totally empowering!"

~ John Abbott, Freedom Entrepreneur.

"An amazing collection of true stories from individuals who have overcome great changes, and who have transformed their lives and used their experience to uplift, inspire and support others."

~ Carol Williams, Author, Speaker & Coach.

"You can empower yourself from the power within this book that can help awaken the sleeping giant within you. John has a purpose in life to bring inspiring people together to share their wisdom for the benefit of all who venture deep into this book series. If you are looking for inspiration to be someone special, this book can be your guide."

~ Bill Bilwani, Renowned Melbourne Restaurateur.

"In the *A Journey of Riches* series, you will catch the impulse to step up, reconsider and settle for only the very best for yourself and those around you. Penned from the heart and with an unflinching drive to make a difference for the good of all, *A Journey of Riches* series is a must-read."

~ Steve Coleman, author of Decisions, Decisions! How to Make the Right One Every Time.

"Do you want to be on top of your game? *A Journey of Riches* is a must-read with breakthrough insights that will help you do just that!"

~ Christopher Chen, Entrepreneur.

"In *A Journey of Riches*, you will find the insight, resources and tools you need to transform your life. By reading the author's stories, you, too, can be inspired to achieve your greatest accomplishments and what is truly possible for you. Reading this book activates your true potential for transforming your life way beyond what you think is possible. Read it and learn how you, too, can have a magical life."

~ Elaine Mc Guinness, Best Selling Author of *Unleash Your Authentic Self!*

"If you are looking for an inspiring read, look no further than the *A Journey of Riches* book series. The books are an inspiring collection of short stories that will encourage you to embrace life even more. I highly recommend you read one of the books today!"

~ Kara Dono, Doula, Healer and Best Selling Author.

"*A Journey of Riches* series is a must-read for anyone seeking to enrich their own lives and gain wisdom through the wonderful stories of personal empowerment & triumphs over life's challenges. I've given several copies to my family, friends and clients to inspire and support them to step into their greatness. I highly recommend that you read these books, savoring the many 'aha's' and tools you will discover inside."

~ Michele Cempaka, Hypnotherapist, Shaman, Transformational Coach & Reiki Master.

"If you are looking for an inspirational read, look no further than the *A Journey of Riches* book series. The books are an inspiring and educational collection of short stories from the author's soul that will encourage you to embrace life even more. I've even given them to my clients, too, so that their journeys inspire them in life for wealth, health and everything else in between. I recommend you make it a priority to read one of the books today!"

"The *A Journey of Riches* book series is filled with real-life short stories of heartfelt tribulations turned into uplifting, self-transformation by the power of the human spirit to overcome adversity. The journeys captured in these books will encourage you to embrace life in a whole new way. I highly recommend reading this inspiring anthology series."

"There is so much motivational power in the *A Journey of Riches* series!! Each book is a compilation of inspiring, real-life stories by several different authors, which makes the journey feel more relatable and success more attainable. If you are looking for something to move you forward, you'll find it in one (or all) of these books."

"I've been fortunate to write with John Spender and now, I call him a friend. *A Journey of Riches* book series features real stories that have inspired me and will inspire you. John has a passion for finding amazing people from all over the world, giving the series a global perspective on relevant subject matters."

"The *A Journey of Riches* series is the reflection of beautiful souls who have discovered the fire within. Each story takes you inside the truth of what truly matters in life. While reading these stories, my heart space expanded to understand that our most significant contribution in this lifetime is to give and receive love. May you also feel inspired as you read this book."

"*A Journey of Riches* is an inspiring testament that love and gratitude are the secret ingredients to living a happy and fulfilling life. This series is sure to inspire and bless your life in a big way. Truly an inspirational read that is written and created by real people, sharing real-life stories about the power and courage of the human spirit."

~ Jen Valadez, Emotional Intuitive and Best Selling Author

Table of Contents

Preface

I collated this book and chose the various authors to share their experiences about how they deal with fear. The eclectic collection of chapters encompass a myriad of different writing styles and perspectives that demonstrate what is possible when we take action and confront our deepest darkest fears.

Like all of us, each author has a unique story and insight to share with you. It might so happen that one or more authors have lived through an experience similar to circumstances in your life. Their words could be just the words you need to read to help you through your challenges and motivate you to continue on your chosen path.

Storytelling has been the way humankind has communicated ideas and learning throughout our civilization. While we have become more sophisticated with technology and living in the modern world is more convenient, there is still much discontent and dissatisfaction. Many people have also moved away from reading books, and they are missing valuable information that can help them move forward in life with a positive outlook. Moving towards the tasks or dreams that scare us breeds confidence growing towards becoming better versions of ourselves.

I think it is essential to turn off the T.V.; to slow down and to read, reflect, and take the time to appreciate everything you have in life. Start with an anthology book as they offer a cornucopia of viewpoints relating to a particular theme. In this case, it's fear and how others have dealt with it. I think the reason why we feel stuck in life or having challenges in a particular area is that we see the problem through the same lens that created it. With this compendium and all of the books in the *A Journey of Riches* series, you have many different writing styles and perspectives that will help you think and see your challenges differently, motivating you to elevate your set of circumstances.

Anthology books are also great because you can start from any chapter and gain valuable insight or a nugget of wisdom without the feeling that you have missed something from the earlier episodes.

I love reading many different types of personal development books because learning and personal growth are vital. If you are not learning and growing, well, you're staying the same. Everything in the universe is growing, expanding, and changing. If we are not open to different ideas and a multitude of ways to think and be, then even the most skilled and educated among us can become close-minded.

The concept of this book series is to open you up to diverse ways of perceiving your reality. It is to encourage you and give you many avenues of thinking about the same subject. My wish for you is to feel empowered to make a decision that will best suit you in moving forward with your life. As Albert Einstein said, **"We cannot solve problems with the same level of thinking that created them."** With Einstein's words in mind, let your mood pick a chapter in the book, or read from the beginning to the end and be guided to find the answers you seek.

If you feel inspired, we would love an honest review on Amazon. This will help create awareness around this fantastic series of books.

With gratitude,
John Spender

"A genuine leader is not a searcher

for consensus but a molder

of consensus."

~ Martin Luther King Jr.

CHAPTER ONE

Exploring the Paradigm Shift in Leadership

By Debi Beebe

Paradigms can be described as structures that have unwritten rules, and they aim to direct actions and beliefs.

A paradigm shift is when one paradigm no longer serves the course of the action plan and there is a need for change—a change in thinking, behaviors and habits.

When it comes to leadership, I think people have a tarnished view-maybe because of someone in their past, someone in the limelight, currently, or even a bad leader in history that hurt a lot of people (ex: dictator). Seeing these poor examples discourages people from going to that place, a place of leadership that allows you to step into the powerful soul you are designed to be.

Not everyone desires to be a leader of something, and those who want to be sometimes have problems understanding what leadership means.

Maybe the paradigm shift in leadership is learning from past mistakes.

Leadership

Before we can acknowledge a shift, we first have to know what a leader is.

Here's the dictionary definition:

lead·er

/ˈlēdər/
the person who leads or commands a group, organization, or country.

Leadership: a **Definition**. According to the idea of transformational **leadership,** an effective **leader** is a person who does the following: Creates an inspiring vision of the future. Motivates and inspires people to engage with that vision. Manages delivery of the vision.

The only paradigm shift I see is that more people are talking about it, without a concept of what it truly is, while we, leaders, are simply just doing it.

Servant leadership

When I met Joe and Kim, I was already married and had two kids of my own.

Joe was 26 and Kim was 22. They were engaged and about to be married. They both had full-time careers but still decided to take charge and lead a non-denominational, non-profit high school outreach program. This was a full-time ministry, and they had big dreams and a big vision of where they wanted this program to excel.

They wanted to make sure the teenagers knew that they could make better choices and stay safe and away from the peer pressure of drugs and alcohol.

Their mission was clear, and they chose other leaders with the same mindset to join them.

Here was their mission:

"Campus After Dark (C.A.D.) is at the center of fostering lifelong friendships, offering support, sharing hope, and creating memorable experiences throughout high school (teenage) years. We have been blessed to come alongside thousands of teens, encouraging and helping them tap into their individual gifts, and enabling them to grow into successful young adults while navigating challenging teenage years."

Providing good, clean, fun and care for the teenager's souls, Joe and Kim were unshakable. This was their mission and their vision. Talk about serving and giving – these two did it completely without regard for whom could or might "use" them. Bad times or good, their nature never changed.

There was a certain time, I recall, where they were going to let go of their own home to fund their non-profit organization so they could keep serving. To my disbelief and my misunderstanding of the bigger picture they had, I tried to stop them. But true leaders ignore naysayers, have a dream, a vision, a deep soul-felt mission and are NOT stopped.

They never saw their greatness, and if they ever did, it would only be through the greatness they saw in others, and again, only because they always treated others as if they were better than themselves. At a very young age, these two were, at the very heart, servant leaders.

3

As I look back over my own lifetime, I think this was my first true glimpse of leadership. There are many different types of leaders, but the story of Joe and Kim touches my soul the most. I learned from them. I learned that leadership is a voluntary position and, with it, comes great responsibility. I formed my own leadership skills by watching them and working with them so closely that I am forever grateful to have ever been around them.

Leader Lesson:

The difference between a good leader and a great leader is that the great leader sees everything along the way as an investment and not a sacrifice.

Leaders know it is an investment and not a sacrifice of their own time, money or life.

Joe and Kim invested in their dream. Their dream was more important than any other thing in their life.

Crowd Breaker Time:

When I first started working with Joe and Kim with C.A.D, I was given tasks that seemed to make no sense. During one of the events with C.A.D, I was running through the crowd of teenagers, waiting for the speaker of the night to take the stage. I watched the high schooler's faces - some were confused, some laughed and I think some were just wondering why they were even there. As I ran, feeling funny and stupid, wondering why it was always me who was given the dumb jobs. "Why me?" I really think, as I reminisce while writing this, that, even back then, I *was* a leader, or I was told I was. You see, that dumb job I had that night was to help the large crowd of teenagers feel comfortable and like they belonged.

This was called a crowd breaker. It was meant to break the ice and allow anyone that felt uncomfortable to relax and be themselves. However, for the crowd breaker that night, I was a streaker! No, I was not naked; I had on flesh-colored tights, head to toe, with a trench coat, and I would run through the crowd and pretend to flash, with the song "The Streak" playing in the background. The purpose was to get a laugh, get the kids' attention and prepare them to be open to listening to the message that night.

The message always had the same underlying theme: to be safe in the choices you make in high school.

It doesn't sound like leadership, it didn't look like leadership, but here's what I learned to be true: If you want to be a leader, you must first be a good, if not great, teammate. Leaders are present, supportive and always have a great positive attitude. You show up no matter what, and, in that case, naked and vulnerable!

OR

How about the time we played a game called "Iron Gut?"

This was a contest designed for kids to win the next up and coming trip, such as water ski, snow ski or any other fun activity!

Don't worry, I know you want to play, so here's how Iron Gut works:

There is a long table with blenders set up and ready to go - with random ingredients such as chocolate syrup, marshmallows, strawberry Jell-O, ice cream, garlic cloves, onions, sardines, and hot sauce. The kids that volunteer to play get to pick and blend three ingredients, drink it down as quickly as possible, and show the closest leader that they have nothing left in their mouth. The first one to complete this wins.

Seems easy, right?

Except, the ingredients were covered, and they had to blend and drink whatever they picked. And the leader? I had the pleasure of checking their mouths and then holding back some of the girl contestants' hair out of the trashcan as they puked. OH, THE SMELL -YUCK!!!!

Let's just say I earned my leadership skills!

This is how bonds are built. When people see the lengths you will go to to help with or lead the vision and the mission, trust grows.

Leaders help build other leaders. Leaders don't want followers. They want to work with and be around teammates. They must be reliable and trustworthy.

After working with C.A.D for several years, I went on to run my own organization, Campus Afternoon C.A.N. It had the same vision and mission, geared toward Jr. Highers! My heart had grown to love the vision of Joe and Kim - C.A.D, which allowed my own vision of implementing the same, but tailored to a younger crowd.

I felt like most high schoolers had already made mistakes they regretted, and maybe, catching these kids at a younger age could head that off at the pass. Plus, I'm not going to lie; I was a little selfish because, at the time, my daughter was just entering Jr. High and I knew she would be a great junior leader right alongside me.

Let me be clear. Although I was in charge, there was a hierarchy to running a non-profit outreach program. Just like in any business, for-profit or non, there is a board of directors that oversees all major decisions.

I would be confronted and have to face challenges on decisions made. It was also during a time when it was unpopular for a woman to lead. Have we changed that yet? Is that the paradigm shift? (Maybe we can have a discussion about that in another book.)

Leaders are willing to stand up for what's right no matter what is thrown at them. They're meant to lead, fight for righteousness and protect their team and teammates because they are our family.

Leaders have to stay strong. Stay truthful. Integral. Stay the course, have the tough conversations and, in this case, deal in a very misogynistic world.

Leader Lesson:

Leaders stay the course.

The payout on the vision always makes it worth it. Being there for the junior high students and the high-schoolers was everything to us who lead those two organizations.

One of my most memorable and heartbreaking times was when I got a phone call from one of my 13-year-old girls, who was alone in a hospital waiting room. She needed me to be there for support, love and a shoulder to cry on because the doctor had just told her that her mom wasn't going to make it.

All of these moments are gifts along our leadership journey. They remind us that we are aligned with ourselves in our vision and our mission. Serving and loving people in times of need is what we all are designed for.

It was my job to paint the vision to keep kids safe, to have fun, to support and to listen. To implore other teammates and leaders to do the same, all for the good of spreading the love of the same mission I was already a part of, and helping Joe and Kim's dream grow.

There are so many cliché terms that I could use for leadership, like, "Captains go down with the ship." You can bet your sweet ass there was no death-wish and the captain did everything possible to keep his crew alive.

"It's lonely at the top." Well, yeah, maybe.

Leaders are protective of who they let in, which leads to, "keep your friends close, but your enemies closer."

A true leader will not allow a dragon to come in and wreck the mission; they'll slay dragons while others complain that their pinky finger got hurt. I'll just say it here: leaders are tough.

Leader Lesson:

A leader cannot falter under the pressure of another person or persons no matter the cost to him or herself.

We must lead ourselves, our day-to-day life. We must have a plan. We must have a vision. Being a leader is a decision. Leadership is a voluntary position that comes with great responsibility; you might get shot, you might get wounded or even risk being killed by the very people who you are trying to help/assist/save or lead to their very best life.

You do not get to give up or quit!

Being a leader is saying things and doing things that most people won't. Leaders take charge. They don't people-please, and they care and love on a deep level.

Leader Lesson:

Leaders come with conviction and get people to do things they didn't believe they could do. Leaders breathe belief. Personally – I love to share my belief in people until they get it on their own. However, I'm human and my belief in you comes with a shelf life. Action is key. Remember that paradigm?

It has unwritten rules that direct actions and beliefs.

The Decision is this:

Whatever mission we are leading, our team, whether one or 100,000, comes first. First before cost – first before anything else, no matter how hard it gets, leaders have to continually move forward. Leaders don't make excuses. (I cringe when people give me excuses.)

Leaders will never ask anyone anything they are not willing to do themselves. Most leaders do more behind the scenes than most will do any day, anytime. As I said, leaders know it is an investment, not a sacrifice, yet they are willing to make sacrifices for the greater good of those within the mission for the vision, the goals, the dreams, and people's lives and longevity. Watch and learn from leaders you admire and ask questions.

People are not leaders because they have power or money; the true leader has or creates a vision, which is always about other people and not themselves.

Leader Lesson:

Leaders understand some will run and some won't. You can still love them, but you must learn quickly to let go of those that don't get it. Because, somewhere out there, another leader is waiting to be born, developed, supported, and they need you, for a moment in time, to believe in them for the leader chain to grow stronger. If you stay around too long, your own chain will rust, and your vision will begin to die. It would be best if you grew new leaders. Leaders build other leaders.

Is a Leader Born or Self-Made?

From the time we were born, we are influenced. We are part of someone's vision. We learn to sell ourselves to be a part of that world and live being told what to do. So exactly how do we step into leadership and not just another manager or boss telling people what to do?

The world's evolution and how our minds perceive it has so many different influences and strategies, old and new. We have evolved within the gratitude space, the growth of ourselves and our individual uniqueness and the allowance of others doing the same. Part of a paradigm shift could be seen as us traveling farther away from militant thinking.

The shift I've seen in leadership is that focusing on gratitude and personal development, first, is the key, and any great quality involves this. It's learning the differences in our personalities, knowing who, why, and what we are and where we want to go with our mission— our true vision.

Leadership is not wavering in our own morals or values. It is attracting other like-minded individuals. As a leader, I look for the beauty, courage and strength of upcoming leaders and teach them skills and beliefs. I did so many things wrong when I was named a leader. If I shared some of my mistakes, perhaps it would help you or someone else, or maybe you'd get a laugh and say, "Yep, I did that."

I joined a network marketing company eight years ago. I thought that I was an adult, successful in business, and no one needed to tell me what to do or how to do it. Red flag! [insert stupid face here] I knew nothing of the network marketing profession. I flailed around and had some success, where others had much more, so I thought to myself, I better get some coaching from a respected leader in the industry. And guess what? My income tripled the second year, and I went on to become a top global income earner within our company. [insert happy face here!]

At this point, I hadn't realized that I had already learned the skills early on from my days with C.A.D and I had to remember what they were.

With our network marketing company, I was building a decently sized team. We were having fun and assisting so many people with achieving a healthier lifestyle and a wealthier one, if they chose to do business.

Then, comes year three. I had a realization. Somewhere or somehow, people decide to name you a leader just because of the money you've made and some of the people you've helped. This is great, but when did we learn the skills needed to be a leader?

In the world of leadership, it's not all about money. People will come and go within your business, vision and mission, but not everybody wants to be a leader.

Was I a great leader right from the get-go? No. Thank goodness for my earlier experiences with Joe and Kim, these skills had been ingrained in me and I just needed to tap into them. I had been taught to show up no matter what's going on in my life. Even if just for one person, it's always worth it. Being a leader in any cause means you have decided to do that/be that. You cannot simply decide, "I don't feel like it today. I'll be back when the mood strikes me." Leadership comes with great responsibility—the responsibility of serving people, and it goes way beyond whether you are in the mood.

Remember, I said leadership is a voluntary position. My role models, Joe and Kim, ALWAYS showed up. They had life happen, just like the rest of us, but they never made a single excuse. I am forever grateful for their impact on my life, my kids' lives and the hundreds of thousands of other teenagers throughout and beyond the city and state in which they live.

Leader Lesson:

Leaders are not perfect. Leaders do not know everything. Leaders surround themselves with the best people.

Here is the top ten list of my leadership "CliffsNotes":

1. A leader shows gratitude for everything, big and small. Within their own life, family, friends and their business, mission and vision. That doesn't mean there are not

lessons along the way. It just means you learn and move on without deeming it good or bad.

2. A leader is involved in personal development on a daily basis. Learning and becoming better, inside and out. Working on the quirks in our own personalities, when it shows up in others, having spent time in our own interreflection, will help someone else. Growing ourselves daily keeps us current with forward movement.

3. A leader understands that not everyone is the same. We deserve, and the people we work with deserve, to be seen and heard for who they are. A leader understands how each person's differences add another dimension to the team, to the vision — for no vision with a mission is one-sided or one-dimensional.

4. The leader does not waver on the values instilled within them and will not compromise their integrity or ask that of another. Have you ever taken a moment to think through a list of the qualities of a leader? Or what type of qualities in a leader you would like to attract? Here are a few of mine: integral, trustworthy, kind, supportive, responsible, unstoppable, visionary, brave, influencer, motivator, belief builder, solution seeker, truthful and honorable; the list could go on and on.

5. Leaders listen. Leaders watch. That doesn't mean that they will change the course over a conversation. However, a good leader will consider a well thought out plan or idea and give credit where credit is due.

6. A leader believes in themselves when no one else does, and in their teammates when their teammates don't see it in themselves, yet.

7. A leader shows up. Does the glamorous and, more so than not, the not-so-glamorous work. To be a great leader, first, you must have to be a great teammate. A

leader keeps their word and if they said they would do something, they do. Integrity.

8.   A leader is courageous, brave and knows when to ask for help. I was told not too long ago that I was a visionary, a true leader. I was shocked to look back and see how much I have grown and stepped into the powerful soul I was meant to be. I had been courageous and brave, and I did learn to ask for help when needed. It gave me a feeling of pride knowing I was making a true difference in the world.

9.   A leader sees the bigger picture and stays on course, not allowing nonsense in life or the stuff that does not serve the cause to get in the way. Is there a true paradigm shift in the leadership, or does the shift happen while staying open and learning to be better, be grateful and let go of our old controlling, non-serving ways?

10.   Leaders are not perfect. Leaders surround themselves with the best people.

Are we born this way? Maybe. Are we made? Maybe. Perhaps it's both. Possibly how we are raised, maybe how we are groomed, the choices we make or don't make. We get groomed more and more with each event in our life and without realizing where or what place we are even being brought to. Then all of a sudden, you get it, just like me as I write these words. Leaders and leadership are some mythical, magical unicorn (that, when needed, will use that horn).

I think there is such a mystery to being and becoming a leader.

What I have described in this chapter is as close as I get to give you what you were searching for. That true definition, that "just tell me how," is not readily or even thoroughly answered here or anywhere else. Why? Because if you are a leader, "the way" is in you. "The way" is you. Vulnerable, naked, running through the

14

crowd, present, supportive, loving, doing what others won't. It's almost private and indescribable.

The way of the leader is, well, not just one way; it is several.

And if you are a leader, it is your way.

What you found.

It's like a secret handshake and one day, I hope to shake your hand.

*** Just to be clear: The above story of the crowd breaker is a parody of American country songwriter Ray Steven's "The Streak."

"A good leader can engage in a debate frankly and thoroughly, knowing that at the end he and the other side must be closer, and thus emerge stronger. You don't have that idea when you are arrogant, superficial, and uninformed."

~ Nelson Mandela

CHAPTER TWO

How to Effectively Lead in a COVID-4IR World

By Izaak Coetzee

Introduction

Most unexpectedly, 2020 was reshaped by the deadly Coronavirus (COVID-19), as its furious widespread effect was felt across the globe. Its unbending impact seamlessly extended across countries, people, cultures, religions, industries and businesses – a tsunami that engulfed all aspects of life.

Without warning, businesses, big and small, found themselves in a vise-grip for survival, having to review their strategic plans while being ushered to re-arrange their well-established patterns of operations. All the impositions that tailed the pandemic's arrival forced a readjustment that nobody foresaw, and no one was prepared for.

The far-reaching impact and consequences of COVID-19 were felt on all parts of business operations, with a significant impact on both leaders and employees. As leaders, we could not continue with business as usual – we had to adapt, evolve with the global chaos, and lead with confidence.

COVID-19 became the breeding ground for a volatile and uncertain world, and unexpectedly directed a gold rush to adopt digital technologies in the workplace. Most businesses didn't anticipate the consequences this would have on employees.

Without warning or time to prepare, this called for true leadership.

The World is no Longer the Same; Neither are We

Across many countries, the rapid spread of COVID-19 resulted in government-enforced "lockdowns" in various forms. This had a direct impact on the way we lived, learned, consumed entertainment and practiced religion, but critically, also on the way we worked.

Irrespective of where you looked, economic erosion loomed as companies, employees and leadership had to adjust to new and harsh realities and consider different ways of doing business.

In the face of blatant challenges in a very uncertain and volatile world initiated by COVID-19, business leaders had to contend with both ensuring business stability and viability, and managing the physical safety and psychological well-being of arguably its most critical asset – its employees.

On the one hand, leaders had to simultaneously adopt a firm, rational approach to protect their business' financial performance, but at the same time, be empathetic towards the plight of employees and the psychological impact of the epidemic on employees. While the aforesaid is nothing new and leaders often have to deal with this on an ongoing basis, the mere scale of the impact of COVID-19 has been unprecedented.

The world, and indeed many businesses, found themselves in an existential crisis, and the uncertainty cascaded to employees. Suddenly, there was a radical shift in employees' priorities away from work to being concerned about personal and family health, accommodating extended school closures and absorbing the human angst of life-threatening uncertainty. This was further exacerbated by concerns employees had about job security and their economic well-being.

It was clear that COVID-19 would directly impact our lives for a couple of months, at least, yet the indirect and unidentified consequences could linger for many years to come.

This has significant implications for leaders as we lead in the present and how we will lead in the future dealing with the trauma of the past.

The Future Became our Present

Before the world was introduced to COVID-19, most businesses were preparing themselves to face the changes that would be brought about by the 4th Industrial Revolution.

The 4th Industrial Revolution, or 4IR as it is commonly referred to, introduces significant change for society, businesses and, specifically, the workforce.

In summary, 4IR uses advanced technologies for the automation of processes, connecting all types of devices and appliances, the use of robotics and data analytics and so much more, all of which will mean less direct human interfaces or interventions.

Klaus Schwab from the World Economic Forum described 4IR as a technological revolution that is blurring the lines between the physical, digital and biological spheres. According to Schwab, previous industrial revolutions liberated humankind from animal power, made mass production possible and brought digital capabilities to billions of people. The 4IR, however, will impact all disciplines, economies and industries, and even challenge ideas about what it means to be human.

Obviously, this would also have extensive implications for leadership and the management of employees.

Fortunately, despite a lot of progress on the technological front, business leaders still had time to prepare for 4IR as it had not fully materialized. Companies and their workforce still had some time to adjust in anticipation of the changes 4IR would bring.

However, this quickly changed at the beginning of 2020 with the COVID-19 pandemic.

The ensuing lockdowns and various forms of restrictions resulted in an unexpected spike in the promotion, acceleration and reliance on digital technologies for work, education and entertainment. New ways of working had to be established, as leaders and employees were forced to work from home and support business operations remotely.

For many, this meant a change from going to an office, plant, factory or shop, to working from home. Unlike before, for various companies, this was not restricted to employees in sales or parts of the business suited for remote working, but to all employees.

The professional lives of many were turned upside down. Technology proficiency and online etiquette around the use of video conferencing tools took center stage.

Demands of work invaded home spaces and often found tenanted in the living room for many employees who were not privileged with dedicated office spaces at home or who had to share homes with large families.

Although COVID-19 ensnared us, we nonetheless were also challenged by so many changes that accompanied 4IR.

For this reason, it feels most appropriate to coin the term COVID-4IR.

COVID-4IR encapsulates the changes birthed by COVID-19 that catapulted 4IR into our lives, making it an undeniable reality. The combined effects of COVID-4IR will continue long after the pandemic has dissipated.

The Consequences of COVID-4IR

The concept of remote working or working from home is not new, and indeed, is often described as a potentially positive outcome of 4IR. This, however, remained a solution for only a minority of the workforce.

In 2020, almost the entire world went into some form of lockdown, and virtually overnight, remote working would become a much needed and often imposed norm.

Suddenly, leaders were tasked to find new ways of working, and "business unusual" became "business as usual," which forced the implementation of technology to be fast-tracked to digitize the workforce. In short, we went from the snail pace of digital transformation to warp speed as COVID-19 fast-tracked 4IR.

Astonishingly, even those who believed 4IR wasn't for them unanticipatedly realized the value and convenience of e-commerce, online shopping, and remote working in periods of lockdown. A new mindset and behavior were crafted - attending church meant watching the service via Zoom. Going to a concert meant watching a band or performer live streaming from their homes. Attending an important business meeting meant never leaving your home.

Amidst all the apparent gloom, leaders were braced with new insights. Many operational obligations continued to be met; meetings, training sessions, conferences and even product launches continued without employees having to leave the comfort of their homes, often accompanied by the benefit of great cost savings to the company. Many employees realized that they could save a considerable amount of time by not traveling to work, and many will find it difficult to go back to unproductive traveling time.

COVID-19 left a path of destruction which touched every part of our human existence, much like a tsunami. Yet, uncannily, it also cleared the path for the acceleration of digital transformation and 4IR. Without strategizing - COVID-19 became the driving force for 4IR.

Even though many are still debating the "new normal" and whether we will go back to our old ways, there seems to be a consensus that we won't simply return to our old ways of working anytime soon. Especially after the positive impact and influence of 4IR technologies has been demonstrated - you simply cannot "unsee" that which you have seen.

Also, the definition of a job and the workplace changed fundamentally by remote working and work from home policies. For many and albeit outdated, a "job" was defined as supervised attendance at the workplace, which fails to hold true anymore. This is paving the way for a new challenge to measure, monitor and manage performance.

Incontestably, COVID-4IR prompted a different approach to leadership.

Leadership Challenges

Even though business impacts and challenges were evident and more predictable, the challenges governing people were less so. How would employees deal with an almost overnight and semi-permanent change in the workplace?

How would family lives be altered, and would productivity over the long-term increase or decline when employees worked from home?

How would employees deal with the loss of human and personal touch?

How would employees deal with all the simultaneous uncertainty and volatility of their personal, societal and work environments?

Most employees welcomed the announcement to work from home until such time that the threat had been mitigated. It soon became apparent that this solution also outlined a myriad of new leadership challenges.

Having to work in a domestic environment, where employees were prone to many interruptions including the dog barking, children vying for the attention of their parents that are on a video conference and worst, a family feud in the background while the manager is speaking to his team about conflict resolution and teamwork.

Over time, employees spoke about feeling isolated and missing face-to-face or personal interactions. Another critical challenge was the disrespect of "time" - work and personal time boundaries became more blurred with many managers scheduling meetings in early evenings. It became impossible to find the work-life balance as advocated in so many self-help and business leadership books.

It is evident that our ability to communicate and express ourselves also became severely hampered. It is often said that verbal and non-verbal communication is an essential part of how people interact and communicate with one another. It is further argued that people rely more on non-verbal communication (65%) than actual verbal communication. This non-verbal communication includes body language, facial expressions, eye contact, posture, gestures, movement, and tone of voice.

While video conferencing as a tool is obviously available, in practice, most people prefer not to have their cameras and video functionality on during meetings. Again, this is driven by a feeling of intrusion of private space, relaxed dress code, and general anxiety of just being on camera. In fact, my estimation is that 80% of meetings did not rely on video, as participants in meetings would be presenting slides or documents with no video of all the participants in the meeting.

This is clearly a leadership challenge as we have just undermined our main ability to communicate, using and relying on non-verbal communication.

In fact, almost all leadership models developed over the last 50 years assume face-to-face interactions between leaders and their people.

The loss of personal interaction and physical contact has left us feeling more isolated, despite the fact that technology has enabled us to be more connected.

Our current leadership model is not fit-for-purpose for COVID-4IR. While there are some fundamental leadership building blocks that will remain relevant and indeed need to continue, we need to ensure that our leadership style can address the challenges brought forth by COVID-4IR.

A New Leadership Paradigm – The 5 Cs for Success

Over the past few decades, changes in the workplace have been relatively gradual and incremental. Therefore, leaders had the luxury to prepare and adapt to changes mostly by utilizing their experience or by learning from other leaders around them.

However, over a few months, we have seen an unprecedented scale and speed of change, which has become overwhelming for many leaders. Leaders' traditional role in anticipating change and then making effective decisions are challenged in a world that consists largely of fear and uncertainty at an extreme level.

Notwithstanding the fact that we all indeed know what good leadership looks like, the increased pressure from an uncertain and volatile world can very quickly and unconsciously cause leaders to adopt unhelpful behaviors.

In many instances, we have lost our ability to listen to non-verbal communication cues. For example, we are denied the opportunity for eye-contact as our eyes are glued to the screens of our multiple tech devices often not seeing the person we are communicating with.

And as we adapt to feeling more isolated, the clarity of our message is tainted. While most people intellectually understand the benefits and importance of collaboration, being isolated (physically or emotionally) potentially impedes our efforts to collaborate.

What can we do as leaders in this new, radically different world?

To address this, leadership development should be redesigned to focus on the 5 Cs for leadership success.

The 5 Cs can be summarized as:

1. Connect
2. Communicate with clarity
3. Collaborate
4. Coach
5. Commit to change

Connect

In the advent of 4IR, many new technologies allow us to stay connected with others. Despite an increase in available communication technologies, our ability to truly connect seems to have diminished. Connecting means so much more than just being in the same room or being in the same online meeting. You may be present, but this does not necessarily mean that you are connecting with colleagues. Often, meetings have been jam-packed with people having other commitments and jumping between meetings. There is an urgency around efficiency and getting on with meetings. However, an unfortunate casualty in the "let's get to the solution" is personal relationships and interaction.

In other words, we get through many meetings, but we do not get through many "connections."

What can we do as leaders to connect?

There's no need to reinvent the wheel. Instead, brush up on some basic interventions to assist leaders and their teams to connect.

Connect with one individual during the start of each meeting- have 2-3 minute conversation on developments in their personal lives, challenges and even celebrations. Express sincere interest in colleagues and developments in their lives. Practice applying this approach with different individuals at each meeting.

Inform colleagues of your availability for engagements/ discussions replacing the old cliché of an "open-door policy." Encourage colleagues to have at least one virtual coffee session with a co-worker where people are literally having their coffee or sandwiches simultaneously, albeit at different locations.

Increase time and staff meetings where workers have a "platform" to connect. The meeting can start as a general meeting, but then later break into 2-3 separate breakaway sessions to connect in smaller groups for 5-10 mins.

Guided discussion themes can be included in these sessions.

An important theme that can be used directly or indirectly is to facilitate staff to connect to the "why." Why is the company pursuing its purpose?

Why do an employee's personal involvement and contributions matter?

Communicate with Clarity

It's been interesting to observe how video calling is often a preferred technological choice in connecting on a social level. However, often the video functionality is disabled at the start of or later during business meetings. This results in a significant degree of non-verbal communication being lost in a business environment. Though this doesn't pose a problem in sporadic/fleeting instances, it gives rise to a new set of challenges once it transitions to being the norm.

When communication is not clear, there is bound to be increased uncertainty and confusion, setting the stage for misunderstandings, conflicts and decreased productivity.

Over time, poor communication will eventually result in lower productivity and reduced efficiency. Apart from the clear impact on the profit line, it lowers morale among employees and inhibits collaboration.

What can leaders do to improve communication?

Constant communication and reminders will become more important in an uncertain world to create increased certainty and trust. This could include giving employees "inside" information - like the company's direction and the challenges that the Leadership Team is facing.

It is recommended that leaders aim to improve communication, both in terms of quantity and quality.

The effectiveness of communication should be encouraged by promoting video functionality – for people to observe verbal and non-verbal informational cues. Randomly question meeting members on their understanding of the key issues or prompt discussions – thereby keeping everyone alert and avoiding creating space for the passenger syndrome (i.e., online people who are present but not participating in the discussions).

Encourage colleagues to summarize key discussions or action points before closing the meeting. Provide an opportunity for questions or clarification at the end of meetings, leading to clarity on the "next steps" and the assigned responsibilities.

During the main meeting, also promote virtual breakaway meetings to encourage greater communication and provide opportunities for small teams to deliberate and provide feedback.

Another effective tool leaders can adopt, which I have used very effectively in coaching and leading teams, is the CPR model. Most people are familiar with cardiopulmonary resuscitation (CPR) as a lifesaving technique in emergencies, such as a heart attack or near drowning.

My inference is through my leadership style to spur effective communication that covers the three parts of CPR.

CPR is a very easy acronym to remember and to incorporate into your leadership and communication approach. I have trained many of my managers and coaches to use CPR when they engage in meetings or even when they are just writing emails or memos. This is even more relevant in situations where there is pre-existing or potential scope for conflict or misalignment. It covers three basic areas of good communication, namely content, process, and relationships.

1. Content – Ensure that content is accurately presented and appropriately crafted for the audience in terms of the level of detail. Stop to assess if there is an overload of detail, and whether it addresses the level of comprehension and interest of a specific audience, including the next steps to be discussed.

2. Process – Ensure that you are adhering to the correct process in sharing the content. Don't use big meetings to ambush or "show-up" colleagues in front of others. Also, don't escalate without exhausting all options.

3. Relationships – Ensure that you have involved all the appropriate stakeholders. Deliver the content in such a manner that

it will build relationships and/or respect, even if there is disagreement on the proposed recommendations or the options.

Do not ignore the power of storytelling. People love to tell their stories. This can be experiences, lessons or insights. Bolster a culture among your teams to share their personal stories, and look for insights into how these may be relevant to current challenges the teams or business may be facing.

Collaborate

The world as we knew it has changed; this will remain true for some time. The dawning realization asks for a reassessment of the implementation of old leadership styles in this transitional phase. What previously served leadership well may not be a good fit under the current context- nudging towards the realignment drawing board.

While COVID-4IR has brought and continues to bring changes to our world, the assumption of immediate adaption in the world arena remains a grey area. It is often said that it is not organizations that change, but rather, people.

Therefore, if you want your organization or business to be more responsive to the changes and challenges brought about by COVID-4IR, you need to establish real engagement with employees on the change process and collaboration on the way forward. With high levels of uncertainty, accompanied by information influx, data analysis, defining options, and identifying possible solutions before arriving at the most optimal solution will be critical. Undoubtedly, this summons increased collaboration.

Collaboration is a critical building block to creating both a sustainable as well as a competitive advantage. Paramount to collaboration is that employees feel that their views are recognized, valued and implemented. Warranting the need for the workforce to express their opinions paves the way for a well-adjusted organizational re-adaption, which echoes differentiated leadership. In the new world of significant complexity and uncertainty, collaboration will become increasingly important to succeed.

The rules of engagement have changed, with market conditions continuing to be volatile and unpredictable. Too often, knowledge and expertise tend to reside in silos within businesses, and very few organizations operate under a prevailing tendency of full collaboration.

It is apparent that due to COVID-4IR, leaders will be confronted with situations they have never encountered. There is a clear indication that the collective leadership wisdom, through a diversity of ideas, must take center stage. More than ever, it's fundamental for leaders to harness the knowledge, skills, experience and multiple points of view of the people around them. Leaders should embrace collaboration beyond lip service by encouraging their teams to steer clear from the silo mentality.

Leaders should further effectuate a culture of collaboration through intentional focus and effort, as it will not develop without visible leadership energy.

Therefore, it's essential not to reduce collaboration to a soft HR issue to encourage teamwork. Leaders must unequivocally champion collaboration as a competitive advantage in a COVID-4IR environment. Collaboration should assuredly be accepted as a strategic capability in parallel with other pricing, marketing, product and other business strategies.

Although technology can enable collaboration, organizations must avoid taking a myopic approach, like thinking that technology application tools inevitably lead to collaboration.

One of the unintended consequences of poor communication is that people easily fall into the trap of focusing on people rather than on problems or correctly identifying solutions. Uncertainty and poor communication also further impede collaboration.

In summary, leaders should:

- Promote, support and, indeed, reward collaboration

- Highlight potential interdependencies and synergies between teams, which could benefit from collaboration

- Reinforce teamwork rather than functional expertise and individual success

- Give employees more responsibility, not just more tasks to do

Coach

Now more than ever before, leaders will have to play a crucial role in leading their teams through challenging times. Teams will be exposed to more uncertainty and various stresses, and it is expected that each individual will respond to stress differently. We are still likely to see that over an extended period, individuals and/or teams could display a lack of motivation, decreased productivity and/or limited communication caused by various forms of internal conflicts.

Leaders' resilience and resourcefulness will be cross-examined; it will be expected that they do more than just leading by example.

Successful leaders are required to add coaching to their skill set and leadership style.

Historically, coaching has been privileged to only a select group of talented employees as part of the talent management process - typically conducted by an external and certified coach. Though coaching has a wide scope, most of it aims to raise employee engagement, personal satisfaction with life and work, and the achievement of personally relevant goals and productivity in general.

Unlike the traditional supervisory role of controlling and monitoring employees, coaching is a collaborative process that can lead to a discussion of goals and help identify opportunities for improvement to reach those goals.

It is not the manager directing the employee, but rather asking probing questions to help the employee take full ownership and accountability. Therefore, coaching employees is about creating a shared understanding of what needs to be done and how it is to be done. This is also different from the normal authoritarian approach where business leaders direct, but is rather a collaborative process with the employee to set both performance expectations and stimulate employee growth.

A coaching leader should help employees work through workplace conflicts and emotional issues, and improve performance and results by focusing on identifying solutions to problems. The leadership coach will also help employees become aware of their strengths and weaknesses and use self-reflection to learn from their mistakes.

As a coach, leaders should work with their employees through the potential risks and uncertainties they face, and assist them in adapting to changing work conditions and circumstances. This also includes helping employees to take personal responsibility for their mistakes, problems and decisions.

A technique that coaches often use, but which does not need extensive training to use, is the GROW model, an acronym for "Goals, Reality, Opportunities and Willingness." The GROW model can be used in both professional or personal aspects of the employee's life, and leaders can use this model to guide their team members. Here are four simplified steps in implementing the GROW model:

Step 1 – Set concrete and precise "Goals." In setting goals, it is also very useful to use the technique or concept of setting SMART goals. This means that your goals should be Specific, Measurable, Achievable, Realistic and associated with a specific Timeframe.

Step 2 – Understand the current context or "Reality." In essence, having a deep understanding of the current reality will provide insights into what you need to do to achieve your goals.

Step 3 – Identify "Options" that are available to achieve the goals. This should include identifying as many options as possible, without discarding some options. Often, taking an unconstrained view can lead teams to discover possible solutions that can be tailored to the situation.

Step 4 - Be very clear about what it is that you "Will" do. This is your action plan in pursuit of your goals. At this stage, you will evaluate your different options and then decide on which option is your preferred plan.

It should be noted that the underlying tenet for any coaching relationship is trust. There should be mutual trust between a manager and the employee, and the connection should be on a personal level, despite the hierarchy.

In summary, the guidance that leaders give should stimulate positive change and growth. Of course, this guidance comes disguised as a set of questions rather than giving instructions and should draw on the insights that employees have.

Although a collaborative approach can be challenging for many leaders, the outcome holds value to an organization aiming to boost productivity and improve performance in uncertain times.

Other simple actions leaders can take include:

- Becoming more self-aware of the leadership choices they're making and what drives their thoughts and actions

- Appointing an internal motivational speaker to share insights

- Leading by example in coaching teams

- Encouraging supervisors to coach their teams

- Reminding teams of company values to guide ways of working

- Using the concept of "golden arrows" - engage employees with a quick bonding event at the beginning of weekly meetings. Pick one employee and allow the rest of the team to give compliments or throw golden arrows (positive statements) about this person.

Commit to Change

Leaders have to ask themselves:

Am I involved in change, or am I committed to change?

Commitment to change encapsulates the other 4 Cs as previously discussed. Real leaders act out their words - they are not just interested in change but actually drive change. They are sincerely connecting with people and communicate with employees in a way that brings clarity and certainty. They are leaders who are truly committed to collaboration and growth, and coach their teams.

Commitment speaks to leaders who embody their leadership style to be open to discovering new ways for growth and development. They don't look at growth and development as something other people should be doing, but look for growth in their own leadership style.

Their commitment is further enhanced by even the smallest changes reinforced daily in support of goals.

According to Vince Lombardi, "Most people fail not because of a lack of desire but because of a lack of commitment."

How do leaders ensure that they stay committed?

1. Ensure that your beliefs and values underpin your commitment

2. Dedicate time to focus on your commitment (for example, set time to connecting with people)

3. Share and communicate your commitment to your team – this will make you feel accountable to your team.

4. Celebrate small wins and successes – be aware of your energies

5. Don't be discouraged when you sometimes fail – adopt a growth mindset, which means that failures are nothing but lessons

While implementing the 5 Cs is not easy, your commitment to growing from failure will help you achieve your goals and become a differentiated leader who can lead throughout COVID-4IR.

Conclusion

"Never let a good crisis go to waste." Winston Churchill's words have never been more relevant than today as we experience the life-changing consequences of COVID-4IR.

Now more than ever, we, as a society of leaders, have the opportunity to reassess, rethink and reset our outlook and leadership styles. This begs the question: will you explore this time to reimagine the future and your role and approach as a leader, or will you see this as merely a pause and try to re-enter a place of comfort you know?

The proposed leadership framework outlines that resilient leaders should take specific steps to identify core qualities and capabilities that will serve best in the current crisis and set the tone for the future.

Some may be convinced that their current leadership model is impermeable and choose to bounce back to the previous status quo. COVID-4IR has handed you an opportunity to review your leadership style to assess its relevance for today and tomorrow. Somehow, this positively stretches your leadership comfort zone and pushes your boundaries to lead and positively impact your team, company and society as a whole.

Successful leaders will draw from past experiences, but make sure that they sincerely connect with their teams, communicate with clarity, promote a culture of collaboration and coach with integrity. This must be supported with a commitment to change through fostering learning, growth and ongoing development.

With the right mindset and a revised leadership approach, both leaders and their teams can emerge stronger to deal with an increasingly agile and adaptive world.

Irrespective from which perspective you look at it – leadership will never be the same again.

**"Integrity is the most
valuable and respected
quality of leadership.
Always keep your word."**

~ Brian Tracy

CHAPTER THREE

The Five Pillars of Leadership

By Kim Wen

A leader is a person who can organize, inspire and direct a group of people to achieve a particular goal. By its very nature, leadership is a highly complex dynamic. We can see this by looking at leaders and examining how they accomplish their missions. Some try to entice people to follow them, while others inspire with love. Some leaders create detailed plans, while others are intuitive. Some project humility, while others are grandiose and expect to be revered.

All leaders share one thing in common: they can tap into and unleash people's energy to work together toward the desired outcome. While some leaders are born with this ability, many others develop it over time. They begin as ordinary people, but they see an opportunity and rise to the challenge. They discover that they enjoy the responsibility of leadership, and they seek more of it. As they emerge as leaders, people begin to perceive them as such, and the feedback loop begins: the more a person is *seen* as a leader, the easier it is for them to *be* a leader.

Regardless of the particular situation or point in time, there are five common traits, or pillars, that all influential leaders possess. These pillars have a special synergy that, when combined, produce the transformative results we value from leadership.

1. Mission

Every leader must have a goal, which he or she helps their followers to attain. The goal, or mission, may be tangible, like building a bridge or sailing across the ocean to a destination. It may also be intangible, like achieving happiness or more success. When the leader is directing an organization, to bring everyone together, the organization must have a written mission statement that is available and visible to all. It is the unifying message against which potential actions can be measured. Those actions that support the mission should be taken, while actions that do not support the mission should be discarded.

Here are a few compelling mission statements that create the special synergy between leaders and their employees and other stakeholders.

JetBlue: "To inspire humanity — both in the air and on the ground."

JetBlue is a major American low-cost airline. The first thing you'll notice is that this mission statement doesn't explicitly refer to the airline's core business: to fly people from one airport to another. Instead, this statement goes beyond its everyday operations to focus on how their service makes their customers *feel,* both about the service itself and in their daily lives. The goal of JetBlue is not to only transport you physically from one place to another, but to uplift you, and they can do this by making what could be an unpleasant, arduous journey into something that showcases the very best of what humanity has to offer. Their sights are set not only in the short term, but in the long term as well.

TED: "Spread ideas."

TED Conferences LLC is an American media organization that posts talks online for free distribution. TED talks are known for being short, concise and wide-ranging in their subject matter. As with JetBlue, you will note that this mission statement does not explicitly say *how* the organization intends to spread ideas, only that it is the organization's goal. Nor is it judgmental; it does *not* say, "Spread ideas that we think are good." All ideas are worth considering, even if many are dismissed quickly as being too radical or impractical.

It is also interesting to note that the word "spread" is an active verb, implying deliberate action. It is not enough to merely tolerate or accept the existence of new ideas; one must take action to disseminate them so that they can touch as many people as possible.

Nike: "Bring inspiration and innovation to every athlete in the world.*

*If you have a body, you are an athlete."

As you know, Nike, Inc. is an American multinational corporation that is engaged in the design, development, manufacturing and worldwide marketing and sales of footwear, apparel, equipment, accessories and services. Their mission statement would be prosaic if it were not for the footnote. A cynic might assert that the added phrase, "If you have a body, you are an athlete," is just a ploy to make the company's market as large as possible and sell their shoes not only to athletes, but to regular people as well. However, the statement is empowering by saying that every human is moving, and by proceeding on that course, we can seek to accomplish something. It is also inclusive in the sense that while many people cannot be "athletes" in the professional sense of the word, anyone can push themselves to excel and do better today than they did yesterday.

Again, note the use of an active verb, "bring." The organization does not merely accept inspiration and innovation. It seeks to be an agent of their dissemination.

The idea that an organization's mission should be holistic was driven home to me one evening when I was with a group of twenty entrepreneurs near the summit of Mt. Kilimanjaro in Tanzania. It was late in the day, and we were seated in a circle, contemplating the sunset. As the sun slowly slipped under the horizon, with a sense of sudden enlightenment, I understood how our fragile earth spins on its axis while making its never-ending journey in a circle around the sun, which is at the center of our solar system. I thought about how a circle can encompass a wide territory. It's important to be in the center of the circle, which is the most balanced and most accessible position from every other point on the circle. Leadership, and the pursuit of the mission, requires you to be in the center of the circle and for that circle to be as large as possible.

From the point of view of a single individual, your circle of concern might begin with yourself and your family. As you step into leadership, your circle widens to include your business and your community. It might then grow wider to include your city or state, or perhaps the entire nation. A true leader is at the center of a vast circle.

If JetBlue had merely said their mission was to fly people from one airport to the next, their circle would have been tiny, but they made a bigger circle for a deeper impact. If TED had said their mission was to present 18-minute lectures, that would have been a small circle. It would be the same case if Nike had stated their mission was to help athletes run faster. Instead, in all three examples, the scope of their thinking was more encompassing, and, as a result, their mission circles were bigger. The essence of true leadership is the willingness and desire to see the big picture, be at the center of a big circle and help the organization and its stakeholders positively impact our world.

2. Responsibility

Responsibility is the second pillar. Leadership is not just a title; it is the assumption of significant responsibility. As the number of lives a leader touches increases, the more responsibility the leader has, and the higher the moral standard required. In other words, the more responsibility a leader has, the more *selflessness* is required. The standards set by the leader will become behavioral guidelines for others to interact with other humans, nature, the earth, and even heaven.

A leader must be willing to dedicate their life to a righteous mission even if no one else supports it. They must be ready to accomplish it alone. For example, consider the boxer, Muhammad Ali. During the height of the Vietnam War, Ali received notice that he had been drafted into the US Army. He told the Army he was a conscientious objector and refused to be enlisted. He was systematically denied a boxing license in every US state and stripped of his passport. In April 1967, Ali appeared outside the Army induction center, and there he handed out a statement:

"It is in the light of my consciousness as a Muslim minister and my own personal convictions that I take my stand in rejecting the call to be inducted. I find I cannot be true to my beliefs in my religion by accepting such a call. I am dependent upon Allah as the final judge of those actions brought about by my conscience."

His actions prevented him from pursuing his profession from age 25 to 29, which are usually the prime years of a boxer's life. It wasn't until 1970 that his boxing license was restored. He achieved enormous global success and became a respected "elder statesman" for human rights.

Leaders need to create a cultural transformation of "No Complaining and No Blaming." Pointing the finger at others actually disempowers the leader. When a leader implements their mission, "I will be responsible" should be the No. 1 attitude. Once a leader holds this attitude, they are empowered.

Playing the "blame game" moves the leader out of the center of the circle and throws the organization into a state of imbalance. It is no longer in harmony with itself or its stakeholders. The most successful leaders can step outside the blame game, admit mistakes, and focus on fixing rather than blaming.

A shining example of a transformative leader is Mary Barra, the CEO of auto giant General Motors. She has spent her entire career at GM, having entered the company in 1980 at age 18 as a co-op student employee. At that time, her job was to inspect hood and fender panels. This was when GM ruled the automotive world. Still, dark clouds were on the horizon. In that same year, the company, which for decades had been one of the most profitable giants in American industry, reported a loss of $763 million. It was GM's first full-year loss since 1921. The truth was that, by 1980, GM had become bloated with waste and inefficiency. On the GM building's entire 14th floor in Detroit, Michigan, insulated from their employee's and customers' day-to-day realities, a tight circle of pampered executives had long avoided reality and responsibility.

Meanwhile, Mary Barra worked her way up through the ranks. In 2009, she was named vice president of global human resources, but the company was rotting from within. In November 2008, CEO Rick Wagoner had flown in one of the company's private luxury jets to Washington, DC, to ask the US government for bailout money. Lawmakers saw the use of the jet as a sign of cluelessness, and for his next trip, a chastened Wagoner drove a GM SUV.

On June 1, 2009, GM filed for bankruptcy.

As for Mary Barra, she kept doing her job, and, in January 2014, she was named CEO of the reformed General Motors—the first female leader of a major automaker. She had her work cut out for her. After just one month on the job, the GM ignition switch scandal—which had been festering unseen for decades—made headlines. On February 6th, GM recalled 800,000 of its small cars due to faulty ignition switches. The scandal widened, and, eventually, GM recalled 30 million cars worldwide and paid compensation for 124 deaths.

By all accounts, Mary Barra has confronted GM's long-hidden faults with unblinking honesty. Her influence has been rising; in April 2014, Barra was featured on the cover of Time's "100 Most Influential People in the World." In 2015 and 2017, Barra was number one on Fortune's list of Most Powerful Women. She has not been the perfect leader—no one is—but she was just the person of humility and integrity that GM needed after its long demise.

Perhaps the most famous leader who made a point of accepting enormous responsibility was US President Harry S. Truman, who famously had a sign on his desk at the White House that read, "The Buck Stops Here." He made some public comments about the sign. In an address at the National War College on December 19, 1952, Truman said, "You know, it's easy for the Monday morning American football quarterback to say what the coach should have done after the game is over. But when the decision is up before you—and on my desk, I have a motto which says, 'The Buck Stops Here'—the decision has to be made."

For Truman, the weight of responsibility was particularly grave. In the closing months of the Second World War, he was informed of the atomic bomb's existence. On July 25, 1945, he wrote in his diary, "We have discovered the most terrible bomb in the history of the world. It may be the fire destruction prophesied in the Euphrates Valley Era, after Noah and his fabulous Ark." In August of that year, Truman had to personally sign off on the dropping of two atomic bombs on Japan. In Hiroshima and Nagasaki combined, as many as 250,000 people died.

In an address in Milwaukee, Wisconsin, on October 14, 1948, President Truman said, "As President of the United States, I had the fateful responsibility of deciding whether or not to use this weapon for the first time. It was the hardest decision I ever had to make. But the President cannot duck hard problems—he cannot pass the buck. I decided after discussions with the ablest men in our Government and after long and prayerful consideration. I decided that the bomb should be used to end the war quickly and save countless lives—Japanese as well as American."

Every leader should be grateful to be spared such immense, life-and-death decisions. But when they arise, great leaders accept responsibility.

This is not to say that leaders disregard responsibility in small matters—even down to the words they speak. As noted by British Wartime Prime Minister, Winston Churchill, "I am your servant. You have the right to dismiss me when you please. What you have no right to do is ask me to bear responsibility without the power of action."

3. Wisdom

In ancient Asian culture, teachers were leaders. To qualify to teach others, you needed first to achieve a certain level of personal enlightenment. This enlightenment meant that you were deeply connected with an inner power beyond your intellect.

As Confucius said, "By three methods we may learn wisdom: First, by reflection, which is noblest; second, by imitation, which is easiest; and third by experience, which is the bitterest." In our current world, by "Googling" a topic, you can gather all the information you need on it, but it is not good enough to be your teacher. Why? Only those who have tapped into the source of our real power can be the teacher or leader.

True freedom creates true equality, and true equality will result in true democracy. If you want to understand what true "freedom" means, only those with eyes of wisdom can really see.

Wisdom is a constant force, focusing on one thought. Wisdom can be explained in quantum theory. There are many examples, including the Dalai Lama, Eckhart Tolle, and Sadguru, who have acquired this attribute from spiritual practice.

Knowledge and wisdom are two very different things. Many leaders have excellent experience, but they misuse it, and most do not cultivate the right kinds. Knowledge without a solid moral and ethical foundation can be dangerous. It is like giving a loaded gun to a drunk guest at the party.

There are two types of knowledge, and they are both very different.

Explicit knowledge, which managers tend to rely on, can be measured, codified and generalized. You can count your money and arrive at a precise number. You can see that the sky is blue or the rain hitting your window.

Ancient people were astonishingly good at observing the world around them. Many Egyptian temples were constructed so that a single ray of light would penetrate a series of openings to illuminate a sacred chamber within the exact moment of sunrise on the summer and winter solstices. Similar precise alignments with solstices can be found in ancient temples in Cambodia, India, Europe, Central America and, of course, at Stonehenge.

While these ancient builders had tremendous explicit knowledge of astronomy, they had no understanding of the universe's underlying structure. For the most part, they believed the sun circled the earth, and that cosmic phenomena—things like comets and eclipses—were attributed to the gods' magic or actions.

Possessing only explicit knowledge can expose you to significant risk. For example, before the Global Financial Crisis, financial firms and mortgage lenders thought they could manage enormous risk with knowledge alone around the world. They did this using numbers, data and theoretical formulas, instead of making judgments about individual loans. The same held for the US automobile industry, which throughout the late 20th century and up until the 2008 crash, relied on offering financial incentives rather than understanding customer needs.

Tacit knowledge takes the bigger picture into account and gives weight to context. This concept, attributed to Michael Polanyi in 1958 in *Personal Knowledge*, posits that analyzing data and having detailed knowledge of it is meaningless unless you consider the broader circle, including people's values, goals and interests, with the power dynamic among them.

Tacit knowledge is acquired first-hand and is not easily transferable. Examples include: speaking a language, riding a bicycle, painting a picture, playing a musical instrument or exerting leadership over a group of people. These activities require a body of knowledge that is not always known explicitly, even by expert practitioners, and which is difficult or impossible to articulate in words.

In contrast to knowledge of any type, which is amoral, wisdom is generally considered morally acceptable. Why? Because human beings, who are usually optimistic, believe that someone who truly understands the world and has wisdom will use it for humanity's benefit. We say that Confucius, Gandhi, and Abraham Lincoln were wise men. They were not perfect—no one is—but they used their wisdom to benefit society. On the other hand, despite their considerable skill at leading and manipulating people, we never say that Hitler or Pol Pot possessed wisdom. The term "evil genius" might be used, but never "wise man."

Paradoxically, wisdom sees its own imperfections and shortcomings. Albert Einstein once said, "Wisdom is not a product of schooling but of the lifelong attempt to acquire it." This ongoing process is lengthy and arduous and instills in the "seeker"—for that is what the person is—a deep sense of patience and humility.

As Socrates said, "I am wiser than this man, for neither of us appears to know anything great and good. But he fancies he knows something, although he knows nothing; whereas I, as I do not know anything, so I do not fancy I do."

Achieving personal enlightenment is challenging and, once attained, wisdom logically follows.

4. Capability

Imagine you are walking along the shore of a big lake, and you meet a man who has a small boat. He says to you, "I'm going to take this boat across the lake!"

You look at the boat, and you say, "Does it have a motor?"

"No," replies the man.

"How about a sail?"

"No," he says.

"Oars, or even a paddle?"

"No."

You are perplexed. The man seems intelligent, and he knows where he wants to go, yet his boat lacks the capability to get him across the big lake. (As for the man's wisdom, that may also be in doubt).

We live in the real world. It's a world of energy, motion and substance, where thought alone does not produce results. Being a good person and having good ideas is not enough; to be of value, they need to be expressed in ways that are accessible to other people. If you have a new idea, you need to be able to communicate it to others. If you invent a new technology, you need to be capable of making it real and able to be replicated.

Your capabilities comprise your skillset. Perhaps you are an excellent public speaker, or you're a doctor or know how to build houses or possess insights into human behavior. Ideally—because you are wise—your vocation will match your capabilities. For example, suppose you are good at managing people, proficient in finance, and are interested in fashion. In that case, you might be happy if you were the CEO of a fashion retailer, like Nordstrom or Macy's.

Capability comes in two forms.

Innate attributes. These are the skills and traits you are born with. This is your inborn talent, and a trait that is "innate" is intrinsic or inherent to a person. An innate quality is core to a person and remains relatively stable throughout one's lifespan.

Your DNA carries lots of information, and everyone has at least one aspect of excellence in at least one area of their life.

Innate skills tend to last a lifetime. An individual who takes an aptitude test once and then retakes it five years later should receive a relatively similar result. These relatively constant innate qualities can help identify a personality match for certain roles.

For example, most humans have the innate ability for language. This ability occurs in all humans naturally. While the details of language use need to be acquired (that's the other type of capability), the impulse to communicate by imitating what adults say is common to most people.

Other innate skills present in varying degrees in most people include the desire to make order in our environment, curiosity and the urge to discover, striving for competence through repetition, and the need to find a place within a social structure.

Innate attributes are not distributed evenly among people. The desire to keep learning and take on more and more responsibility is not found equally in everyone. Many people are happy to "coast," and, to paraphrase Earl Nightingale, author of *The*

Strangest Secret, to "tiptoe through life, hoping to make it safely to death."

Acquired skills. As children, our innate skills are not enough to keep us alive, much less thrive. A five-year-old child left to fend for himself in nature would not survive. During adolescence and even into adulthood, we are intensely dependent on the acquired skills taught to us by our parents, teachers and peers.

We learn acquired skills from many sources. At school, we learn how to read, write and complete arithmetic calculations. School also teaches us about human behavior and how to get along with teachers and peers. At home, we may learn how to care for ourselves and how to cook and clean. At work, we learn job skills. In a religious setting, we can be informed about spiritual matters, which we then embrace or reject.

As you can see from your experiences with other people in everyday life, your innate aptitudes will dictate how aggressively you seek to add to your acquired skills. Some people are eager to learn, while others don't care. This difference is a reflection of the most important innate attribute of them all.

Attitude is the wild card, the x-factor. Your attitude is a function of how you see yourself in the world. If you see the world as an exciting place where you can be successful and make a difference, you will have a positive attitude and will strive to become a leader in your field. If you see the world as a dismal or unfair place, you will be more likely to have a hopeless attitude and accept a life of mediocrity.

While your attitude is an innate trait, it can be changed, for both better or worse. An adverse event, such as being terminated or getting divorced, can damage a positive attitude. On the other hand, a negative attitude can be slowly repaired to become positive.

For example, a nation's military seeks to transform ordinary people into leaders. This transformation is undertaken step by step, and, to an outsider, some of the steps may seem small. When a soldier or recruit wakes, the first thing they must do is *make their bed*. This must be completed according to the specifications of the particular branch of the military. It's a simple task that anyone can do. Why is it important? Because it has a profound effect on the soldier's *attitude*. Recruits come from a wide variety of backgrounds, and many may have low self-esteem. Making your bed correctly is a simple task that does not necessarily take much time, but once it's done, the recruit is left with a positive feeling of accomplishment. It's a small success, and if other small successes are repeated throughout the day, the recruit's attitude can change from "I am a loser" to "I am a winner—and possibly even a leader."

A leader's positive attitude multiplies their talents and skills to create a synergistic result, and the outcome is greater than the sum of its parts.

The result is Permanent Peak Performance (PPP). This is a state in which capability meets mission, responsibility and wisdom to produce the fifth and final pillar of leadership.

5. Integrity

Integrity manifests itself as a consistent and uncompromising adherence to strong moral and ethical principles and values.

Why is integrity important?

The Five Pillars of Leadership work in harmony; each supports the other. Together with mission, responsibility, wisdom and capability, integrity contributes to excellence in leadership. As Samuel Johnson, a clergyman, educator, linguist, encyclopedist, historian, and philosopher in colonial America said, "Integrity without knowledge is weak and useless; knowledge without integrity is dangerous and dreadful."

Integrity informs the leader's decision-making and personal behavior and provides a standard against which their actions can be measured. A leader knows when they are honest or dishonest. They know when they are acting in the best interest of others or themselves and applying the rules unfairly or fairly. By choosing to act with integrity, life becomes much simpler. Deception increases stress, and deceptive people must constantly worry about being exposed.

A leader's integrity is vital to their employees, customers, board members and other stakeholders. Honesty is key. Employees want the truth, not a "spin." If the business climate is challenging, they want straight talk. Suppose a business needs to innovate and change direction. In that case, stakeholders are much more likely to support the new direction if they believe the leader is acting in the company's best interests.

People want to work for ethical leaders. They know that if their leader acts with integrity, that leader will treat them with respect and do what's best for the business. Companies with management teams that work with integrity enhance their ability to attract investors, customers and talented employees.

In contrast, stakeholders dislike hypocrisy. Too many leaders do not practice what they preach. They will announce the company needs to "tighten its belt" and cut expenses, but the leader's private jet and top executive "retreats" to island resorts are somehow deemed essential. The leader proclaims a new era of innovation, but new ideas from employees are either stolen or ignored. The leader issues a memo reassuring employees that the workplace is free from discrimination, yet women are still paid less than men.

Such a lack of integrity is corrosive. When employees and stakeholders see hypocrisy, they think, "Why should we be honest? We are just being taken advantage of. We can cut corners, too." Product and service quality suffers as employee engagement declines.

"As I have said, the first thing is to be honest with yourself. You can never have an impact on society if you have not changed yourself. Great peacemakers are all people of integrity, of honesty, but humility."
~ Nelson Mandela

Integrity encompasses the biggest circle. True integrity means the leader is not concerned only with the small circle—their personal fortune, or the results of the next quarterly profit report that will keep stock analysts happy—but with the larger community and nation's circles. The leader with integrity acts not only to strengthen the organization, which is necessary, but to bring the most good they can to the greatest number of people.

Integrity is a vital part of oneness and the common good. Once a person's spirit, mind, emotion, body, and energy are in alignment, they naturally become the creation's source. They self-lead, have the power to create and empower others to do the same.

We are all interrelated. Integrity allows us to become one, and achieve oneness and the common good.

Integrity is practiced quietly. Humble leaders who have integrity are rarely written about because they avoid the spotlight, and what they do, from a news cycle perspective, is almost boring. Think about the famous corporate scandals that have been in the news. In 2001, Enron collapsed after it was revealed that company leaders fooled regulators with fake holdings and off-the-books accounting practices. Five thousand employees lost their jobs, and shareholders lost $74 billion. And there was Bernie Madoff, who bilked his trusting investors out of an estimated $65 billion. Some integrity breaches are not directly related to the quest for profits, but involve the company culture, such as the 2017 scandal at the ridesharing company Uber. Here, it was the sexist workplace climate that revealed a lack of integrity. The outcry led to the resignation of CEO Travis Kalanick, and a new CEO, Dara Khosrowshahi, was brought in to clean up its image and create a new culture.

The media is full of such stories. Meanwhile, the tens of thousands of CEOs with integrity, who guide their companies to a year after year of both profit and community acceptance, work quietly without grabbing the headlines.

A leader with integrity considers his or her position to be a privilege, not a right. It's about recognizing that many good ideas will come from other people, learning from both your own mistakes and those of others, and being able to admit when you make a mistake.

Mission, responsibility, wisdom, capability, and integrity; when brought together in a spirit of humility and service, the Five Pillars of Leadership can help you be an instrument of positive change in the world.

"Positive leadership uplifts everyone, all it takes is you: The best version of you."

~ Unknown

CHAPTER FOUR

Leadership, A Being of Gratitude

By Stefan Almér

I was in my office when I overheard a conversation, or, I would say, one person yelling to another in the office on the other side of the hall. They were arguing about deliveries that were late in the project we all worked on. I could hear that the guy being yelled at felt very bad about the situation and that the guy who was yelling was upset and frustrated, something the current situation in the project could make us all feel. The argument continued for a while and ended when the guy being yelled at gave up and said, "Ok, ok," with a dejected voice. The guy that was yelling turned around and walked away without a word. After a while, I went over to my colleague (the guy who was yelled at) and asked how he was. He looked at me with hopelessness in his eyes and said, "I'm ok, I just feel that I can't manage my workload right now. It's too much and the pile is just getting bigger." I stood there in silence; he did not seem to want to talk anymore, and I got this strong feeling not to say anything more right then. I said, "I'll be in my office if you want to talk."

I went back to my office and continued with my work. Ten minutes later, my colleague came over and sat down at my desk. He said, "I just want to say how much I appreciated you coming over to ask how I was." He continued, "Actually, it's you who would have the biggest reason to yell at me, cause it's your deliveries that have the biggest delays, but you don't yell. Instead, you ask how I am and if you can do something for me, and you do that often." He added, "I will make sure to catch up," which he did! I was quite stunned by getting the feedback; it came directly from the heart and touched mine. I felt a warmth inside, and I could just say how much I appreciated him, too. It was a moment where hearts met in silent understanding.

My small act of compassion was that I acknowledged his humanness and vulnerability. I stood by him. I gave space. He could be just what he was in that moment, and it seemed like it helped him find his spirit again. Then, he knew how to prioritize; he knew what to do. This situation happened early in my career and it taught me something about heart-centered leadership. There and then, it made me understand compassion and empathy. What I figured out later was that the deeper energy I felt at that moment was gratitude and that gratitude has a big role in being a leader.

As managers, we usually spend our time parked in our mind box with our focus on the outside, trying to figure out the next step, the end result, or the strategy. We get lost in performing the tasks of today because we believe we have to; we have to perform and meet neither ourselves nor the other in our humanness. If we spent just a minute tuning in a little bit deeper with ourselves and the other first, our leadership would be much more empowering. As an effect, we would perform our work easier, and it would be more fun because we would find ourselves feeling more appreciated.

Gratitude is empowering. When we feel gratitude deep inside, our being becomes empowered. We emit appreciation, which affects our actions. I say that when the energy of gratitude runs the heart and mind of a leader, her actions will become an act of kindness and grace. Her words will be empowering, and decisions will be sustainable. She will not take more than she needs. Greed no longer drives her. Her need for power, position and wealth will fade, and social responsibility will start to rise. Her empathy will guide her to have a clear perspective. She will not put others in unnecessary danger, and, if she has to, she will know that it has a higher purpose and that it's a necessity. Her success will not harm anyone or anything else, because in her heart, she will know how to use the position of power she's been given.

In the next few pages, I will share my story and thoughts on leadership. My leadership career has been a significant part of my life, has taught me a lot and had a big role in my consciousness of gratitude. It's an appetizer to a deep topic, and it's a story of bridging the gap from duality to oneness and bringing together leadership and being from the heart. It has been an awakening process within an ordinary life, with some great insights along the road.

Our path is made by our being and the choices we make; I have made crucial choices in my life and I have wished for a lot of things, preferences and wishes that I did not envision the consequences of, them. When I was young, I chose to explore my own potential, whatever that could be. Somehow, on the way, I found leadership or leadership found me. I can say it's been an effect of my being; I have not been able to sit still and keep my mouth shut. I had a lot of ideas and was willing to take responsibility and ended up in leadership roles through many parts of my life. When I started to work in leadership roles, I saw a new dimension of human interaction that made me curious. I somehow found my purpose, chose to explore and be an outstanding leader.

When we make choices and start to live by them, reality will send situations with possibilities and challenges that we need in some way to benefit or learn from, to mature, to realize and to get insights into something new. Our ability to navigate this beautiful chaos, inside and out, is what unfolds our potential; that's our self-leadership.

My navigation, my path, has not been a straight line. At least, my experience, on the inside, has been a mixture of success, struggle and self-doubt, somehow trying to accomplish both different missions and my own becoming. When I was young, I asked for enlightenment and I have been given everything along the road to wake up. It just took me time to realize and embody that everything that got in my way, even all my struggles, were gifts to make me wake up and mature more.

This has made me realize that the boldest choice to make as a leader is not to make decisions of things outside our self. The boldest and most courageous act is to take a long good look in the mirror, take a big breath, turn inside to see which part of ourselves we let control our actions and start to be aware of that part, maybe even change it. Is it fear, greed, envy, survival, or is it compassion, peace, joy and love that we let control our being, and how we relate to the situation we are in?

Do we, as leaders, choose to look upon our colleagues, circumstances, and ourselves with gratitude- the gratitude of being right here, right now- given the possibility to co-create? Or, do we choose to let our ego run the show - colleagues are stupid, can't do anything directly, argue to put ourselves in the best position and maybe think that our way is the best? By using brackets?We don't care about what will happen to the other as long as my voice is heard, my opinion is obeyed, or I get the bigger paycheck.

Do we choose to walk the path of oneness, joy, gratitude, creativity, innovation, co-creation, and win/win, or do we walk the path of duality, debate, conflict, fight, greed, and win-lose? Are we aware, daily, of which part of us runs our show? We have all of this inside, but what do we feed ourselves and our reality with? What do we want to define our being with, what's our preference? In the short term, we can make the same results, but in the long run, I believe there is only one path to create sustainability.

The good leader; A friend of mine once said, "A good leader for me is someone who dares to be who they truly are." I replied, "I'm working on it," and he smiled and said, "when should you stop working on it, you can't work on being. Either you are, or you are not. The more you try, the less you are present in your being."

I had found it challenging to be a good leader when, on the inside, I was pissed off with things not turning out the way I wanted. Standing the pressure and stress, meeting my own insecurity and still being who I wanted to be solidly grounded in the heart was a challenge. It's a challenge that can be overwhelming, exhausting, and it can ruin our energy. When under pressure, our defense strategies start executing, and if it continues, it's easy to become hard. Anger might come momentarily, but hardness does not come instantly. It accumulates; it comes creeping with the traumas and stress we encounter on our path. Though, we can choose to park ourselves in the state of our illusions that made us harder in the first place, and continue to fight and get even harder. Maybe until we do not recognize ourselves, anymore. Or, our aching heart can't bear it anymore, and we wake up and realize that there are other ways of being. We can be heart-centered, ourselves and exceptional leaders, all at the same time.

That moment with my colleague, I realized that everything is about people and how we, as humans, use our self-leadership to relate to the situation and each other. I had started to realize that the only one I can and do lead is myself, and that it is who I am and my being, what I emit, not really what I do, that made a difference. At the time, I could not put words to it, though I just knew. I knew because the better I led myself and the more my colleagues felt appreciated and treated like the professionals they are, from the heart, the more fun we had, the better we cooperated, and then we would excel in what we did together.

I have found that leadership is not a role we can be assigned; it's something others make us. It's an effect caused by our being and our ability to lead ourselves. It's the followers who turn someone into a leader, and how we embrace our followers will be crucial if they continue to follow and we can co-create. We cannot tell anyone else to be something they don't want to be, at least not without force. Then, they will not be it anyway; they will just pretend to please. People are only loyal to what they have chosen themselves and have embodied, their own belief and story. We only have full power to change ourselves, so when leaders embody gratitude, compassion, and empathy, they encourage others to appreciate it.

The power we have as a leader is given to us by those who make us their leader. The leadership role can influence, inspire, and empower, or we can use it to manipulate, control, and dominate. It's up to every one of us to be aware of and choose our path. There are many leaders and several through history that have had many followers doing very nasty things. So, there has to be something that defines if we will be known as a "good leader." Those I think of, like Dag Hammarskjöld, Nelson Mandela, Mahatma Gandhi, Winston Churchill, Eleanor Roosevelt, Rosa Parks, Martin Luther King. I think they all had a being with a strong spirit or what I would call "a big heart," a big heart with a lot of gratitude. Those are the ones I think history has presented as good leaders, that is my preference!

The essence of leadership; From the day we are born, we are supposed to behave in some role or another, as a child, parent, partner, student, or manager. Most roles come with a history and an imaginary costume, in some way. They come with a heritage; someone has acted in that role before and has built-in expectations, values, and energies into the role or position. We may be unaware of this due to not having taken it on before, in which case, we will either continue and repeat it, or change it with our own identity.

Take the lead role as it so many times has been defined. The leaders are the heroes throughout history, and, in today's society, they are the winners of the battles, have all the privileges and power, can influence and have a good life. It's something prestigious to be a leader. The leader is supposed to show the way, point out the direction and take responsibility. The leader should have courage, be strong, firm, fair and collected, and know what to do in every situation. The leader should be in command and control of the situation. There is not much talk about gratitude or the leader being anxious, vulnerable, soft, loving or just plain human. Pretty often, we put the leader on some kind of pedestal, and if they don't fulfill our expectations quickly, we will pull them down or let them sit there and point fingers at them. The leader is the one to blame.

But this is just an illusion, something we have made up, something that we chose to believe in and continue to repeat. We must let go of everything we have made up about leadership. I think the essence of leadership is our ability to be present and how we, out of that presence, lead ourselves concerning everything and everyone. in every situation, making use of the power we've been given. Reality will respond by either making us the leader or not.

How well we lead ourselves depends on how much we dare to be what we truly are, not to act out of some theory, role, with a mask, a costume, or attributes. Just pure naked and vulnerable as we are, and, with that, we have to take the risk of losing our face. It's actually our softness and our vulnerability that will make us manage the hard days. To be secure from the heart and make difficult decisions in a complex and rapidly changing world demands softness with the self, which demands gratitude. So, if gratitude has been of importance to good leadership before, it will be of even greater importance in the future. I believe the future belongs to leaders who choose a truly heart-centered being.

Growth of gratitude and maturity; I had made a fundamental choice and dedicated myself to becoming an exceptionally good leader, and to explore my full potential.

When my career took off, I wanted more. I tried hard to live up to all the illusions of the leader: I read a lot of books, went to a lot of courses and tried to become the living example of all the words. As time went by, I lost track of the trust in myself and the intuitive leadership I used in my early career. For many years, I used all the leadership techniques and practiced my inner work. I did all the exercises, meditated, worked hard and was mindful, but I did not find what I was looking for. Through all the frustration, I did not recognize that the path I was on was a slope in the wrong direction.

I had a self-image that I was a well-educated and a good leader, and I kept that self-image up and have been rewarded for it. But the more I "worked on it," my skills and my way of being just didn't work out anymore. The more honest I was, and the more I tried to do the right thing, the more it seemed to go in the other direction. It felt like I just kept banging my head against the wall. I got more and more frustrated, I became irritated and short-tempered, and I did not recognize myself anymore. I literally felt sick of the suit I was wearing, both the imaginary and the physical. I looked in the mirror and saw a different version of myself than I used to see. My life played before me like a movie on the screen, and I did not like what I saw. I had become painfully aware of my shadows and had forgotten that which I knew in younger years.

I have struggled a lot, being angry with life and thinking that life was unfair to me. Even though I am spiritual, I was also pretty good at messing up my own life. I was not especially grateful neither for myself nor for my life, but I tried keeping the façade, not showing what was going on inside. There was always something to do where I could hide, and I kept myself busy. I mixed up my own identity with my work, and in my stubbornness, I tried to change the reality to satisfy me, not accepting the reality as it is and instead choosing a different path or circumstance for myself.

When I gave up trying, my turning point was to surrender and open up to be, and feel conscious and aware from my heart, not my mind. From that point on, it became easier to breathe and my energies started to flow easier. I felt extremely vulnerable, but I received an increase in clarity and unquestionable intuition that gave me strength and a clear intention. There was only one path ahead: truth.

For a long time, I had a struggle jumping back and forth between duality and oneness but have realized that when we dedicate our being and actions to our heart and tune in on the pure frequencies of gratitude, joy, love and courage, change happens—our character changes. Our truth, values, and beliefs will change, and so will our actions and the reality we live in. It's the choices we make, what level of energy we dedicate ourselves to on the inside, which will make a difference.

One of the insights this gave me was that we might think that maturity comes with age or by taking responsibility, which is true to some extent. However, age and responsibility provide a limited effect on maturation. We actually mature when we vibrate from purer frequencies; that's when we awaken more and more and our conscious expands. That's maturity. Age is not a guarantee for that, but it helps. It gives us time to learn from the choices we make and the situations we encounter in life. The more we tune in, the stronger our relationship with our true self will become, and the better we will lead ourselves and the better leaders we will become.

Inner work; To be good leaders, we need to fill our own cup first, and we need to be mindful of what we fill it with. Second, the only one we actually can change is ourself. Inner work is, therefore, of importance in any kind of leadership, in particular, if we have an official role where we are supposed to be leaders or influencers to other people, and even greater if we are leaders to leaders. The more significant the role, the higher the importance.

The inner work I have experienced is the most important, and it is to open up to remember what we truly are. The first step is to tune in with our heart space and get an increased awareness. For this, I have found meditation to be one of the most powerful tools. It helps us to be more present and aware, to be more patient, tolerant, and peaceful. It opens us up for a new understanding and being. Doing heart-centered meditation for ten minutes every morning helps to act from our heart-space as clear as possible, to be ready to create the day together with others and to bring harmony to the moment.

I meditate every day and try to make my daily routines a ceremony of gratitude from the heart, doing them intentionally. This can mean doing something practical, like watering a flower, making the bed, cleaning the desk or charging the laptop, even the smallest things to honor the things that support us.

I also do something to honor and pay gratitude to my body and spirit. We can do whatever we like, but be intentional about what we do and make it a ceremony. Work out, dance, do yoga, qigong, bicycling, play an instrument, paint or whatever to really feel our spirit and pay gratitude to our body and its ability to support us. It's not the action but how we connect with our self that is of importance.

When we tend to our lives intentionally with gratitude, life tends to us back.

STAYFUN; Today, I know gratitude is a fundamental base for authentic heart-centered leadership, and from that, comes pure joy, courage and humbleness. If we can't embody gratitude for the honor and power we have been given from another to be their leader, we are not their leader yet; we are still just "a boss." I have been blessed with a life of opportunities, and I have understood that each person or situation we encounter on our path is a gift, a portal to a deeper understanding of myself. Today, I can embrace what I meet from the heart and with gratitude.

I have chosen to STAYFUN. To me, that means to choose wisely from my heart what brings joy and harmony to my life and to others, to share joy, co-create, be creative and go for win-win. It's a peaceful living. It's essential to stay present, be aware of my choices and what parts of the inside of me make me do them in every moment. I know that my self-leadership and my use of the power I have been given will create my reality.

This makes me humble. Gratitude is something I am; it's a part of me, just like love, joy, frustration, and anxiety. It's a frequency that lives in me and through me. It's a part of my being, which I can choose to be tuned in with or be distorted too, just like a radio channel.

During this process, I do believe I have become a better leader or at least better at leading myself.

The essence of good leadership, as I think it always has been, is to act out of a pure heart and remember that we are all human and have our flaws. It is not always so easy to live up to, but we can try. Even though it might be scary to take that big breath, I have not heard of anyone yet that has made the move and wants it

71

undone. Our character has nothing to do with the "clothes" we put on; it's how we wear them that matters. The mature leader wears his, or her, leadership in balance with his feminine and masculine aspects. He does that when he comes to a true understanding of his vulnerability and finds his true strength, in his heart.

The way of the leader is to be present, and aware of our being and the effects that cause; it's a choice we make. As I have found, the essence of heart-centered leadership is a being of gratitude. When we speak uplifting words and inspire others from our hearts and with our presence, then we ignite the spark of gratitude. That's why I say that when the energy of gratitude runs the heart and mind of a leader, her actions will become an act of kindness and grace. Then, we empower the good stuff.

The present and the future belongs to leaders who dare to be vulnerable and vibrate with gratitude. Being truly heart-centered makes their voices heard!

"The challenge of leadership is to be strong, but not rude; be kind, but not weak; be bold, but not bully; be thoughtful, but not lazy; be humble, but not timid; be proud, but not arrogant; have humor, but without folly."

~ Jim Rohn

CHAPTER FIVE

What Is Holding You Back as a Leader?

By John Spender

The new wave of leaders inspires others through their actions. They are collaborative and exude a warmth that endears and attracts people into their sphere of influence. Their team wants to be around them, learn from them, and support their vision. They create environments that naturally foster progression, which encourages everyone to be an evolved version of themselves. All but gone are the days of totalitarian leadership in successful companies. The new paradigm of leadership is a form of collaboration where the leader guides the task and project to completion. The leader generates a compelling vision that inspires others to join, and in turn, they bring their complementary skill set to the table. In this new leadership style, as your opportunities increase to empower your team or "collaboration partners," it's important to continuously grow your perception of yourself. This is why the average CEO reads 60 books a year. They are expanding their knowledge and their own self-image. Leaders of the new paradigm must grow and expand to remain inspired to place themselves at the forefront of their industry. An organization's vision is only as strong as the leader.

In the new paradigm of leadership, you don't always have to look to the CEO or the head of an organization; rather, it's a common perception that everyone, no matter what role they play, is a leader on some level. Whether you are the leader of your household, workplace, or leading yourself to align with your values or commit to the tasks you set yourself. Why? Because becoming an inspiring leader is a learned habit; it starts with menial things. "How you do anything is how you do everything." It's a belief in doing the right thing because it's the right thing. No one will follow a leader for long if they aren't aligned with their leader's integrity.

Life can propel us forward faster than the mind is prepared to handle. We live in a world of information that is ever-increasing and readily accessible. Naturally, we are easily consumed by immediate gratification—the "I want it all now" mentality. It's easy to find yourself in a leadership position without having a grip on what life has handed you, mentally and emotionally. We approach leadership by saying yes first, then figuring out the details as we go along.

Moreover, if you don't appreciate what you have, you won't know how to be its steward, which often results in losing what you've got. This is exactly what happened to me in my first landscaping business. I had completed my first year of a four-year apprenticeship as a landscape gardener with the council in an exclusive district with pristine landscape gardens. I was keen as mustard, showing up to work early with an open mind, eager to learn. It wasn't long before leaders within the organization started to notice my work ethic and enthusiasm. One, in particular, had more private work than he could handle. We became friends and worked together on our days off. There was so much work that I decided to leave the council in my second year. I was topping my grades at the horticultural college. I already had experience working part-time as a landscape laborer in my final two years of high school. It felt like the right time to take a chance on myself. As a council apprentice, I rotated to different horticultural divisions every three months. Some of them were not the best of experiences due to poorly-run teams with terrible work ethic. Also, I could earn more working for myself! I had plenty of referral business, and my focus was on doing the best possible job I could do.

Things really began to take off in my third year of business, before I was emotionally ready for it. Having studied horticulture in high school and completing my parks and gardens trade certification, my knowledge base was already strong. I took classes for landscape design three nights a week and landscape construction one afternoon a week when an amazing business opportunity landed in my lap. It was a substantial seven-figure contract to develop parklands in the southeastern suburbs of Sydney. In the blink of an eye, I went from working for myself with one laborer to running a team of 15. We completed the project successfully and more work came flowing in. The opportunities were too big of a leap for me and I worked myself into the ground. I suffered an emotional breakdown at only 24 years of age. I lost all my contracts, my apartment and most of my material possessions. I have written about this in previous *A Journey of Riches* books in more detail. Especially in book eight, *Transformation Calling*, I share in intricate detail what happened during that period of my life. I developed a cocaine habit, paired with mixing in the wrong circles that clouded my judgment. All I had left was one work truck, some tools and a significant blow to my self-esteem. Although I was good at leading by example and attracting talented workers, I knew nothing about successfully leading a team. I lacked the emotional intelligence and experience to handle the pressure that accompanies the responsibility of running large projects.

Rather than approaching the projects from a perspective of collaboration, it was my way or the highway. I was easily frustrated when a team member didn't quite understand my instructions. My approach to solving problems was bullish at best, if not full-blown authoritarian. Back then, I saw it as the "hard, but fair" approach. I paid higher than the average wages and I expected results. At the time, I resented my father for his tyrannical approach to parenting. Now, here I was, displaying the same behaviors in my own business. Once I realized what was happening, over time, I recalibrated the experience seeing both the negatives and positives of my leadership style in the early days. I made adjustments in my preceding businesses. I can honestly say I'm much better now than I used to be. Naturally, the changes didn't happen overnight. It was several years of consistent improvements through my dedication to my own personal growth and evolution as a man. This intense personal growth period in my life of paid seminars, group coaching programs, workshops and books was birthed from my addiction to recreational drugs. I would like to think that I'm a testament that it's never too late to get off the wrong road and right the wrongs in your life. You can be the main lead in your movie because, ultimately, you are writing the script. Changing the narrative is completely up to you.

One recurring theme in this book is that everyone is a leader. If you can't develop the discipline to lead yourself, then attempting to lead collaboratively, you will struggle. It all starts with you. Practicing self-discipline grounds you to your word; maintaining integrity to your word is the quickest way to building more self-confidence and respect from your team members. Even if they don't say it, your team wants the assurance that you've got their back. Trust is eroded when a leader says one thing and does something completely different.

When you say to yourself that you want to be a great leader and adopt a "whatever it takes attitude," then exceed your expectations, you ask for trouble. Here's what I mean by that. In the corporate business world, when you're promoted, you are paid more money while taking on more responsibility. A sales executive makes less money than the sales manager, the sales manager makes less than the general manager, and the GM makes less than the CEO. Why? More money, more problems. They're paying you for problems — for your ability to manage pressure, stress and problem-solving. As the level of responsibility increases, so does the level of pressure and adversity. Your success comes from your preparedness and ability to handle adversity.

If you don't handle your own personal development, stress can be almost impossible to manage. Rather than stepping up to the challenge, it's easy to take the bottle, or in my case, ecstasy and cocaine. But this is no way to build your leadership skills — it's simply a form of escapism. When you refuse to be intimidated and learn how to manage stress within yourself and your team, doors will open up to new choices and possibilities. I've discovered this in publishing books. At first, I published one book a year, then two, followed by four, and then ten in one year! Each time, there was an increase in pressure, stress and also abundance. I learned how to facilitate the production of the books and chose to empower the co-authors and my team instead of commanding them. I found healthy ways to relieve my stress and found mentors to guide me. I was able to replace substance abuse with exercise. By committing to a regular meditation practice, I replaced a reactive and competitive mindset with one of peace, poise and calmness. My "emotional bandwidth" increased, allowing me to feel my emotions and process through them rather than being ruled by them, spewing onto anyone who happened to trigger me.

When you allow your "problems" to grow, you expand your personal development, and there is a magic to life that will come to you. Doors begin to open up for your progression to the next level of leadership. Many people don't take the lead due to a fear of failure; thus, they never live up to their greatest potential. A successful leader sees only the potential in others, inspiring them to reach for more within themselves. As you believe more about your team's capabilities, you allow them to learn and grow as leaders. Most of today's successful leaders have a peer group, mentors and read many books to help them course-correct when necessary. It's not about showing that you can do everything on your own; in fact, it's rare to meet a modern-day leader who doesn't have a support network they can lean on.

After my fall from grace, it took me five years to rebuild myself before starting another landscaping business — working for others, doing more than I was paid for and adding value. This time, I built it step by step, expanding steadily instead of expanding before I was ready. As I worked on personal development, I eventually sold my business and transitioned into life coaching and public speaking. I hired a mentor, developed my neuro-linguistic programming skills and again, I was met with rapid increase, but this time, I was better prepared for it. What made the difference was the work I did to evolve my identity and my beliefs in what I could achieve. I was able to first lead myself by aligning with my purpose before I attempted to lead others. As a result, I attracted clients who were inspired to take action and expand their vision of themselves. When the pressure became too much, I made sure I had an experienced mentor to lean on for guidance.

In the new paradigm of leadership, there is a responsibility for each member of the team to lead themselves, assuring their cup is full and not going too far outside their threshold. Leading oneself is about managing the internal conflict when new opportunities arise, playing your part in the team's collaboration efforts. Naturally, this isn't always smooth sailing with various options available to complete a single objective. It's the leader's responsibility to hold energetic space within the team so everyone can freely express themselves.

The very word "leadership" used to intimidate me. "Me, a leader?" I had a fear of imposter syndrome. Another common fear is that of achievement. It's true! As creatures of comfort, it's easy to get caught in repetition, doing the same mundane things over and over again. I believe, now more than ever, that the new paradigm of leadership calls for transparency, collaboration and a strong sense of self. These traits can bring all sorts of pressure onto a team when things don't go according to plan.

Five Limiting Beliefs that Might be Holding you Back

Following are my five limiting beliefs that may be holding you back from becoming the leader you'd like to be. No matter what capacity or area in life you're seeking to be a better leader, I believe you will find these points useful in adapting an open, collaborative approach to leadership.

1. I Am Unworthy

Feeling unworthy or "not enough" is a common and unhealthy characteristic that drives many leaders to what they believe is success. All the world's material possessions won't change this inner emptiness because the solution is found within. We deserve to have both material possessions as well as worthiness. What often happens is leaders will see opportunities beyond their feeling of deservedness of it. As a result, they reject it or catch "excusitis" to avoid pursuing the opportunity and making the most of it.

I remember driving to Jack Canfield's home in Santa Barbara with my director of photography, thinking to myself, "Wow, I'm really doing this!" I felt way out of my comfort zone on the inside. Part of me didn't feel as though I deserved to be creating this opportunity with such a well-known celebrity. On the outside, I was cool, calm and focused. It helped that I was driving and chatting with my DP, which eased the imposter syndrome and feelings of unworthiness. Slowly but surely, the heavy feelings dissipated, and Jack and his wife, Ingrid, were amazingly welcoming to the crew and me. It's always a significant confidence boost when we can push through our doubts, fears, and self-limiting feelings, especially when faced with a new opportunity or find ourselves out of our comfort zone.

2. I'm Afraid of Ridicule

Leadership requires you to put yourself out there, even if you don't want to stand out from the crowd or be perceived as different for fear of being shot down, laughed at or feeling exposed. Many people have a belief system that causes them to hold on to "being ordinary," which prevents them from taking the lead even when they're competent and qualified. My inner dialogue used to be, "I am afraid I will become a target for being laughed at." The reality is sometimes I did!

My fear of ridicule stemmed from an embarrassing moment on my grandparent's farm when I was about ten years old. One particular afternoon after lunch, I had gone for a long walk looking for yabbies (gray fish) when I needed to take a dump. I tried to hold off so I could go to the farmhouse toilet. When it became apparent that I wasn't going to make it, I went behind a tree. I was a little late and I had crapped myself. I didn't want to face the taunting from my grandma, so I went behind the main dam five minutes from the house and hid my dirty undies under a rock. Little did I know, my older brother had been following me and found my undies. Worse yet, he went back and snitched on me. I didn't get into trouble, but I was teased and made fun of by my own family. They thought it was so funny. It did take a bit of inner work to reframe that experience that I held onto for so long. I thank them now because that was an opportunity for me to build resilience, and I can now laugh about it. Many people unconsciously hold onto things that don't serve them and give disempowering meanings to events that happened in the past. Although my story from childhood doesn't directly relate to being a leader, it demonstrates this idea of building resilience to overcome the fear of ridicule.

As an adult, I can recall launching my first *A Journey of Riches* book. I was proud of my accomplishment and had worked hard to make it happen. Expecting my family's full support, I was shocked to have certain members of my family attack me in disbelief, shooting me down and accusing me of not telling the truth. One even left a negative review of the book on Amazon! As a leader, you have to believe in your own abilities and stand your ground. I believe in being fully transparent for the benefit of helping others. When you put yourself out there and take the lead, you will inevitably become the target for others who don't believe in your capabilities. And guess what? That's OK. If you have the courage to put your fear in the backseat, you will be the example for others who are searching for their own firm conviction, solid values and self-belief.

3. I Fear Social Change

Many people play small throughout their lives and they build a persona for being a follower. Over time, "fitting in with the crowd" becomes safer and more comfortable than taking the lead and standing out. Signs of fearing social change can be fear of rejection, loneliness or fearing people calling you a sellout. When you fear social change, it feels risky to potentially be rejected by your social circle. This happens more often than people realize. Peer pressure and the yearning to fit in continues well beyond high school for many people. The desire to fit in is so strong that people will go against their own values just to please others. Being loyal to so-called friends can cost you your own individual growth.

I saw my brother struggle with this limiting belief. Our Aunty had offered him an opportunity to complete his last two years of school at an exclusive boarding school two hours south in Parramatta, Western Sydney. I was excited for him to take the chance to broaden his horizons and increase his chances of employment after school or university. Academically, my brother was much smarter than I was at the time. I was shocked when he rejected her generous offer. It was me. I definitely would have taken it. After reading all the information about the school, he didn't think it was a match for him. He was afraid he wouldn't fit in. Moreover, my brother didn't want to leave his close-knit group of friends, and they didn't want him to go either.

Leading yourself means staying true to your convictions, stretching your boundaries, and rejecting peer pressure. If you don't, you may find yourself passing up on that promotion or some other opportunity that can move you forward in life.

4. My Success Won't Last

Many people experience a certain degree of success, and although it feels good in the moment, there's a small voice telling you your success will be short-lived. This limiting belief thrives on a lack of belief in yourself. It's as if any past situation that ended in what felt like a failure is doomed to repeat itself. If you suffer from this limiting belief, your internal dialogue might sound like, "I'm not going to take this position because I'm afraid I'll end up losing it in the long run; I might not have what it takes." Or, "I'm not going back to school because I may not graduate." Even in personal life, "I don't want to go out on a date because things might go well, and the last time I got into a relationship, it didn't work out, which caused me a lot of disappointment." The belief that success or happiness won't last will lead you to the point where you won't take any chances on yourself.

Lately, I've been having my own struggle with this limiting belief. I can have a perfect day where everything went smoothly, and at the end of the day, I'm filled with a deep level of appreciation for such a fulfilling, productive day. Yet, in the back of my mind, there is a trapped belief telling me the next day can't possibly be as good as today. I'm at the stage now of simply observing my thoughts around this limiting belief. I'm oscillating between the idea that anything is possible and the law of gravity: what goes up must come down. My conclusion is that with enough momentum of affirming my ideal reality and how I want things to go, things will even out a little. It helps me feel a lot more balanced.

5. I Have to Be Perfect

Perfectionism is one of the most common limiters I see with leaders. If they don't do things perfectly, they will be perceived as a failure. It's ok to be "secretly talented," but stepping into the limelight requires too much risk. Perfectionists become more concerned about the security of their reputation as-is rather than pushing themselves to achieve more.

I remember the first chapter I ever published in the *A Journey of Riches* series. Striving for perfection, I took so long to hand in my draft; it completely halted my progress. This was a case of my perfectionism getting the best of me. It makes me laugh now because I have a fantastic team of editors who can easily steer me in the right direction. To be a successful leader today, we must be able to embrace our insecurities while having the confidence that we can find a way to succeed in spite of them.

The reality is that nobody is perfect. I've found the best approach to overcoming perfectionism is to focus on making progress, moving forward toward your vision or dream and refining things along the way. Mistakes don't negate success; that's how we learn. It's ok to cut ourselves some slack from time to time.

The Mindset of Today's Successful Leader

If you want to be a successful leader and go where none have gone before, you can be sure you'll encounter all sorts of challenges and external pressures along the way to your goals. In fact, when you experience such challenges, you can rest in knowing that you're on the right track and this is all part of the progress of breaking through your fears and limiting beliefs. There's a saying, "If it were easy, everyone would do it." Most people are not comfortable making significant changes and stepping out of their comfort zones, so it's not surprising that they don't like it when others are going where they're afraid to go themselves. The new paradigm of leadership is about clearing self-limiting beliefs and confronting conflict in a confident and strategic way, being an example for your team.

To keep evolving as the new leader of today, yes, you desire to know yourself at an increasingly deep level while also being open to explore any blind spots that you might have, including flushing out limiting beliefs. The vision of the whole is only as strong as the leaders hence the necessity to empower a collaborative approach to tasks, issues and challenges to create unity within a collective. I've learned more from my mistakes in leadership than in any other endeavor in life. It took some time to learn what not to do, understand myself enough to develop an awareness to make adjustments when needed. Above everything is else, if I had to start from scratch again, I would continue to build my inner self and make sure I have a strong team around me with strong mentorship. Once you've reached a certain level of success, it's your responsibility to empower others and your team to their highest level of success in the most collaborative way.

"The task of the leader is not to put greatness into humanity, but to elicit it, for the greatness is already there."

~ John Buchan

CHAPTER SIX

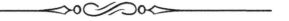

The Leader Within, The Leader of Tomorrow

By Elizabeth Jennifer Chua

Everyone is born with the potential to be a leader, and it begins with being a leader for yourself in your own life.

If you had told me that when I was younger, I would have never believed it. Growing up, I remember being an extremely shy girl, so shy I could never answer a question in class, talk to strangers or even order food if there was a line behind me. This was my life for about 13 years. I understood the concept of leadership and a leader back then, but there was no way that I ever considered becoming one, since I would not even be able to address anyone as a group, let alone lead the team. It was natural to have leaders in school among students, and I always admired how my friends were able to step up to the plate so confidently. Never in my life did I even dare to dream of being in a leadership position.

Why, then, did I choose to be a part of this book, to share a perspective of leadership? That's because, for the next ten years, I went through the three B's. A breakthrough, a breakdown and a breakout. It's been a whirlwind of an adventure that I almost lost my life to, but I managed to come out on the other side not only stronger, but more importantly, more joyful and able to share that and serve others. By no means am I saying that I've got leadership all figured out. But I would love to share this fulfilling life of serving others, knowing that the recipients of my service may also

89

go on to share and make another person's world a better place, along with improving my life and developing as a person while doing so. As crazy as my past experiences were, I would never trade them for the world if it meant giving up what I have and the person I have grown to be right now.

One of my favorite books of all time is *Matilda* by Roald Dahl. To this day, I can never forget one quote from that particular title, "So Matilda's strong young mind continued to grow, nurtured by the voices of all those authors who had sent their books out into the world like ships on the sea. These books gave Matilda a hopeful and comforting message: You are not alone." Words shared by people have such immense power to impact, influence and inspire their readers. Whether I was going through a time in my life where I felt comfortable, stuck in a rut or defeated, those words could always provide a boost, push me out of my comfort zone and remind me to experience life to the fullest in every given moment.

Throughout this chapter, I wish to share some of the stories that helped me discover how the leader within myself is the leader that I needed, and that the world would need, and how that applies to every one of us. That is what gave me the passion for writing this chapter, knowing that I have received something so beautiful that I could share and others, too, could continue to put out more into the universe. This chapter could end up being a nice ice breaker for you to get to know who Elizabeth is, to discover yourself through some of my experiences or to take this as an inspiration to grow further as a mentor. Still, I know that when humans share experiences, we inspire one another and great things come out of that. I am thankful for this opportunity to share my experience with you.

The Leadership that we are Pursuing

What does it actually mean to be a leader? Today, there are numerous definitions of what makes a leader, but dialing it back down to its basic essence, it is the person who guides, leading the person or team toward a goal.

Why is it important for us to have leaders? A life with goals is like being at sea. It includes joy and new adventures, which also entails danger and hardship. Sailing a ship without a captain, the crew might have all the resources and manpower, but the ship could end up nowhere, deserted, or unable to navigate through a storm. That is why many have recognized the need for leaders in our society – not to dictate the direction, but to guide a team toward its destination.

While we acknowledge the importance of leadership, we must certainly talk about effective leaders. We have seen leaders on either end of the scales of leadership, from the likes of Mahatma Gandhi and Saint Mother Teresa, inspirational leaders, to dictators such as Hitler and Stalin. In today's context, being in the information age, technology has improved many aspects of our lives. However, it has also made the world increasingly complex and difficult to navigate, making it necessary for us to have good leaders.

When taking some time to think about mentors in our lives that we associate as leaders who inspire us and help guide us, there could be a long list of different contributions in different fields, leadership styles and approaches. Still, the common factor in these leaders that we look up to is their service out of love. Through the great visions and plans, their passion and love for the people they are leading pilot them to be great leaders. We need servant leaders more than ever in today's world.

91

The question that many would like to answer would be, where do we begin this expedition of leadership, and how do we embark on this journey to serve? I've put together three simple steps that I have taken to kindle the spark of leadership within, so let's dive right into them.

Awakening of The Leader Within

Step 1: Discover and embrace your gift of leadership

The beginning of this journey starts with believing that you have the capability to be a leader. Although all of us have different abilities to begin with, the best place to start being a leader is in your own life, for yourself.

The first of the three B's that I experienced was a breakthrough. After graduating and moving onto my next phase of schooling, a teacher took it upon herself to motivate the sleeping potential she saw within her students. She continuously guided me out of my comfort zone, each time helping me gain confidence in taking up leadership roles. I started wondering if there were any truths to being able to speak up, at least for myself. That itch in my heart led me to take a leap of faith, and it opened my eyes to discover the ability to speak up for myself and guide others, motivating a team to complete our goal.

At this point, I was starting to get excited about the opportunities that came my way to lead in projects where I knew I could be of service. With mentors like my teachers and encouraging peers, I made the conscious decision not to fall in line but to actively decide to embrace leadership. That opened up many doors for me to discover myself and grow into the leader I could be.

Realization is not to be nagged or forced into taking on the task, but truly seeing that sprout inside and knowing that it could grow into a giant beanstalk. This recognition gives us the strength to embrace the leadership opportunities we get in life.

If you have ever looked it up, you would know there are tons of resources and mentors out there to get the ball rolling in our discovery of leadership. However, to embrace the gift of leadership, it has to come through your own free will and choice. You must choose to be a leader for yourself. You can have a million mentors around you planning and carefully executing plans for you, but it would not work out if you're resistant to the idea of being a leader.

Take your time to discover yourself, because you will come to understand yourself best and can make the best decisions for your own life. An important thing to remember in this first step is that taking control of your life does not mean you stop receiving help and guidance from other mentors. Rather, leadership equips you with the skills to carefully consider that guidance and weigh the decisions, in order to make the right choices to lead yourself toward growth.

Step 2: Explore and nurture your gift of leadership

When you start making more decisions for yourself, especially those geared toward self-growth, you will discover some of your personal strengths. Know that those are precious gifts, gifts that could very well be used to enrich both your own life and others. Knowing and embracing the seed of leadership planted in every one of us is definitely the foundation needed. The next step would be to practice honing those skills and talents.

Identifying the seedling of those skills, however, does not equate to mastery of them. You have to embrace them and take steps to nurture those talents. There is a well-known parable of a sower who scattered seeds on different types of soil. The sower had some seeds that fell along the way on hard ground, and those seeds could not sprout or grow at all and became snatched up by birds instantly. The second place the seeds landed was in some rocky place, where there wasn't much soil. The plants sprouted very quickly, but because the soil wasn't deep enough, they withered in the sun. Thirdly, some seeds fell among thorns and although the seeds were able to plant and grow the roots needed, they could not compete with the number of thorns that overtook them. Last but not least, the last batch of seeds fell on good soil that enabled them to burrow deep, grow strong, and produce fruits.

All seeds contain nutrients and energy inside of a hard, protective coating. They all had the potential to sprout beautifully, but only with the right environment and raw material, were these seeds allowed to thrive and grow into a fruit producing plant. Through exploration, we can find the mountains of resources and mentors available to us, and we can most certainly find the greenhouse that can help us grow.

It is important to remember you cannot pour from an empty cup; we, too, cannot give something that we don't have to begin with. My discovery of this step was through my second B – my breakdown. Very quickly, in school, as well as other organizations such as Toastmasters that I was active in, seeing how I was able to handle my work, people began to ask me if I could help serve in different positions. With that newfound confidence and inner need to please others, I pounced on every request that came my way. I was so busy serving that I became unable to improve upon my skills. I found myself limited in my service, which led me to overcompensate with any resources that I had, that I didn't leave much for myself. I insisted on continuing what I thought was expected of a leader for others and I didn't step up for myself. Discovering my potential to be a leader and choosing to serve every cause led to burnout. It triggered a downward spiral – I felt like I wasn't good enough, almost like I was a waste of space. I felt truly defeated, and like I had no purpose because I could not be of value to anyone or anything.

It would take a long time to walk you through the difficult times accompanying my growth journey, but let's focus on the good that came out of my breakthrough: the final B, which was a breakout. I was blessed with many loved ones who helped me break out of that vicious cycle, which tore me apart. They were there for me when I could not be there for myself.

I knew deep down that I was able to be a leader from my breakthrough. Still, it took time and courage to open my eyes and see that there was a whole other journey out there that I had yet to embark on. I needed to be there for myself before I took more steps, to one day be able to help others, too. This new revelation taught me how important it is to plant your seed and nurture those gifts first. Explore the resources available on leadership, practice and improve on your skills, and always decide to take care of yourself.

Step 3: Sharing your gift of leadership with the world

As we are constantly growing and prioritizing our well-being, we would see that there are times when our talents and gifts can be of service to others. To be the leader does not mean to arrogantly assert that you have the highest capability, but to humbly accept this opportunity of sharing your garden of skills and experiences that you have been carefully pruning.

This world, along with everything and everyone in it, is so loved that the opportunity will definitely present itself in our life when we are ready to serve. It gives us purpose and meaning in this pilgrimage of life we celebrate on earth.

Never overlook how much your service could be of help, as Marie Forleo, named by Oprah as a thought leader for the next generation, always ends her YouTube videos by saying, "Stay on your game, keep going for your dreams because the world needs that very special gift that only you have." At times, our fear of not being good enough to be a leader for others may creep up on us, but it helps to remember that your efforts, experiences and results of the growth in that field, thus far, could be invaluable to the other person/team, just like our mentors before us.

After the breakdown, although I had a breakout and started picking myself up and working on myself, it was terrifying for me to take the step to guide others. I kept wondering if I truly could be of service to others. Upon chancing into a career of working with youths, I always worked hard to coach them, but I never thought much about it. Year after year of seeing them grow and hearing from my graduating students how I was there for them and helped them through hard times really proved to me that we all could put a little more positivity out there in the world. It is a fantastic gift that keeps giving, as I watch those youth go out and continue to inspire others.

Bee Movie, released in 2007, follows the story of a bee named Barry, who sues the human race for exploiting bees after learning from his florist friend that humans sell and consume honey. They won the lawsuit, and all the major honey producers had to shut down and return the honey to the bees. With the overflow of honey, the bees didn't need to continue working as hard. They stop pollinating flowers and the plant life slowly died. The world became barren. Thankfully, Barry, with the help of other bees, realized their species made a mistake, and carried out a massive operation to pollinate the world again, slowly coloring the gardens once again.

Like our talents, yes, they could certainly benefit us, but in sharing and being stewards of the earth and others, we can make the world a better place. We find our lives so meaningful, not just because we get to experience the world better for ourselves, but also because we can give that to others.

We are all truly made so wonderfully unique, and the world becomes a better place with every one of us being a part of it. What is more beautiful than admiring your own garden is sharing that view with others, sometimes inspiring them to start their own garden. And, before we know it, we have created an enchanted forest of servant leadership.

Summary

Everyone is chosen and born with the gift of being a leader. It could be for a country, an organization, family or friends, but it always starts with being a leader for yourself.

Never forget that love is the language of the heart, and it is where true servant leadership begins. And that is what we need in our world today!

Leader's call to actions:

1. Discover and embrace your gift of leadership
    a. Take time to learn about yourself and grow into making decisions that are good for your self-improvement.
2. Explore and nurture your gift of leadership

      b. Nurture skills and talents that you have, using the abundant resources available and mentors' help.

3. Share your gift of leadership with the world

      c. Last, but a crucial step to share with others the talents that you have through opportunities that come your way.

I truly believe that every one of you reading this now has the special gift that only you can give to this world, and it would be a pity if it goes to waste. Do not let any moment slip by. Live to the fullest and we will see our world growing in the directions that are not only great for us, but that future generations can enjoy, too.

Remember that, like life, leadership is an ongoing journey. Keep discovering yourself and share your gifts and talents with the world and, in the words of Brain McNight's "Back At One": If ever I believe my work is done. Then I'll start back at one.

Let that inner warrior roar, and let the leader of tomorrow sing. I wish you all the best in your journey of discovering leadership!

"To lead people, walk beside them. As for the best leaders, the people do not notice their existence... When the best leader's work is done, the people say, 'We did it ourselves'."

~ Lao Tzu

CHAPTER SEVEN

The Power of the Space We Hold

By Michelle Gardiner

"I'm not coming out!" "Are you sure? Come on…" "No, I'm not! I refuse!" "You have some really important things to share." "No! I don't care! I couldn't deal with it." "What couldn't you deal with?" "They won't listen to me and I can't handle them not listening to me. It's too much. I care too much, and I just know that they're not going to listen." "Well, they're certainly not going to hear you from behind this toilet door." There was quiet. I heard the flick of the door lock. The toilet door opened, and possibly the gutsiest 15-year old I have ever met was standing in front of me. "How bad is my eye makeup?" "It's actually not too bad," I comforted as I handed her a couple of tissues. "Yeah, I've been crying like a baby. What do I do? I don't even know what I'm supposed to say." "That's easy. Sort your makeup and let's get you ready."

For several years, I co-designed and facilitated a forum where young people who had a lived experience in Out-of-Home Care and Child Protection would present to a panel of Ministers, Commissioners and CEOs about the social issues that they felt needed to change. An audience of around 100 professionals would oversee this dialogue.

This young woman had fled the room just before she was due to speak and had hidden in a toilet cubicle, convinced that those in significant leadership positions would not listen to her, and that despite what she thought was vitally important to share, the room full of people would see her as a "15-year-old kid" who had nothing important to say. Dare I say that this 15-year-old had probably endured more than most adults would encounter in their lifetime and, through this, she had become incredibly resilient and resourceful. She also had a huge heart. She was intuitive, personable, wise, quick-witted and intelligent. In most encounters, she would teach me enough to leave me wondering what my role in her life actually was. While this young woman would often present herself as "tough," on this particular day, she shed several layers and allowed me to see more of who she really was.

I watched this young woman stand up and share, with the utmost depth and passion, about what needed to change in our society for young people just like her. She moved the room in a way that many who had been speaking on huge stages for years could not do. Of the many life lessons that I have gained through young people, one key component would be that the quality of lessons that both a CEO and a 15-year-old have to offer can hold just as much value as each other.

As humans, we all want to feel seen, heard, listened to and included, like our words hold value and to know that they will make an impact. We all want to know that something within us holds substance that will create purpose and meaning in some way that extends beyond ourselves. We all want to feel connected to one another and the higher order of things. In many ways, my varied Child Protection experience will be the backbone to most other things that I do in my lifetime, and for this purpose, I reflect on it throughout this piece.

I would like you to stop reading for a moment. Find an empty container or vessel of some kind. It can be a vase or a glass. I would like you to imagine and play a game of "what if…" What does this container mean to you? How do you choose to value it?

What would you like to put in this container? What if I told you that you could put anything you like in it, however, not an unlimited quantity, as the container can only hold so much. Would you fill it with gold? Would you fill it with dirt? What if it doesn't matter what you fill it with because the contents would only magnify the value you place on the container itself? What if the vessel's value is your perception, as its holder, and that you are deciding how you determine its worth?

What if you believed that the value proposition of the container itself automatically amplified the value of its contents and became a reflection of the container itself. What if creating change were a matter of becoming so strongly attuned to the energy which we bring to the container that we could automatically and dramatically increase the value of its contents? We all own things that hold purely sentimental value. These are often things that connect us to our humanity and life, and we have the potential to place this same power in anything that we hold.

Leadership is said to characterize the motivation, guidance and capacity to influence a group of people. The key denominator here is "people." I am particularly interested in how social change occurs between groups of people across time, and I wish to incorporate a conversation around a "new paradigm" within this. I also believe that "holding space" exists between one or two people just as readily as it does between an entire nation. Often, what we find present in either the micro or macro is also found in its counterpart. Therefore, we are all leaders in our own right and have the potential to create just as much impact within our own sphere of influence as do our most well-known leaders.

To intentionally choose the path of leadership is to decide to stand for humanity and the kinds of environments humanity deserves. And once we feel that we have stood for humanity and moved beyond it, it is our responsibility to open our eyes and to choose this over and over again. Leadership is our capacity to be with and express ourselves and to enable others to do the same. Our job is never complete. We will always have more space to bring more humanity to the surface. We will continually dance in the murky space between confronting our own truth and integrity, and holding spaces that foster trust, belief, growth and fellow human development. To stand in the message of "I will believe in you, until you believe in you" is to marry the space between healing and leadership, that will help both ourselves and others to return home within the unique story that we each carry.

I was once invited to coach a young Aboriginal woman about self-love. The most powerful work that we did together occurred once she articulated her true desire to be a role model by sharing her culture and ancestry, paving the way forward for other young women like herself. From this point forward, self-love was an easy task to address. We all need something to stand for and someone to impact in a way that demands that we take great care of ourselves. Our pre-requisite for being a leader is human. If you can find your way into space, you are worthy and deserving of being welcomed with open arms and having a voice just as impactful as anyone else in that space. Our task is to create more spaces where this is our norm.

While any one of us can impact change in many ways, to distill and be confident in how we, as individuals, can best serve, takes courage. In most situations, I will not be the loudest change activist. However, I strongly support those who choose this path. Our world is deprived of a gentle, yet informed and intentional, approach to change, and this is required as we move into the future. As leaders and space holders, our greatest strength is in our self connection and adaptability. There is something profound about an individual who can be both deeply empathetic and compassionate, intuitive and nurturing, while also being a strong advocate who is prepared to have tough conversations and make great things transpire. Our capacity to be attuned to our inner guidance system, aware of our energy utilization and open to harnessing the learnings at our disposal is where power lies.

Our leadership lessons are scattered for us like trinkets throughout our lives, waiting to be picked up and redistributed wherever they are best served. My growth as a dancer has demanded that I dramatically expand my bodily awareness, inner alignment, self-awareness and my capacity to read, connect with and attune to others quickly. Performing has taught me how to utilize my body, expression and space to expand my presence to capture and maintain a space's energy. Learning to truly hear music has taught me how to feel and respond to energy based on my demands. To dance is to expand and express the nature of humanity and convey a message that replicates my learning to facilitate large rooms of people. Where leadership asks us to become all of ourselves, it also demands that we bring all that is available to us.

Joe Dispenza states that the greater proposition of energy that we can create through elevated heart-centered emotions enables us to experience more wholeness, connection and oneness with others. He also informs us that our heart can create a magnetic field three meters wide. Therefore, to create a higher functioning, more loving, connected, resourceful and creative society, we must transcend lower energetic states of pain, shame, blame and fear. Our capacity to hold spaces that align with love opens the space for greater freedom, self-ownership, healing and choice. This means that the intention that we establish for our space of influence holds the capacity to transform, heal and change our human experience.

Emotional safety and love are fundamental to our survival from birth. With 95 percent of our brain development occurring within our first five years, we spend our lives both confirming and seeking to repair our inherent views of relationships. Bruce Perry, an American child psychiatrist, states, "Fire can warm or consume, water can quench or drown, wind can caress or cut. And so it is with human relationships; we can both create and destroy, nurture or terrorize, traumatize or heal each other. Relationships are the agents of change and the most powerful therapy is human love." Who we are, the energy that we exude, and the ways that we bring one another back together offer us some clues about our way forward.

As a society, we are both more connected and disconnected than ever before. We have seemingly endless opportunities, yet are plagued with fear, segregation, biases, stigma and stereotypes that significantly restrict and isolate many of us. Where our responsibility is to lead a society that is working to rise above these issues and their deeply entrenched social impact, we are asked to hold regard for those in our pockets of influence, where we are too bringing this intention out in them. We are asking that those in our space come to believe in a higher quality of life and humanity and to establish spaces that hold this standard.

This asks that we are constantly checking in on our internal biases and ignorance, and humbly seeking to understand what is unfamiliar to us. We are all inevitably raised with, create our lives around and die with biases. However, we can get better at recognizing, understanding and confronting difference, diversity, injustice and inequality. We can do our best to create truly inclusive spaces and ensure that the messaging we send is embracing of humanity in all its forms. We can all do much better at welcoming rather than turning away. We can appreciate that we will get our attempts wrong over and over again. We can then do our best to understand more, hear more stories and respond better. We will come to realize that homelessness, mental health complexities and abuse are not "out there." We will see how they could very easily be our own story. And in our sharing, hearing and evolving, we will begin to shift the shame, blame and pain that is the undercurrent that we all experience, in some way.

Several years ago, I sat in a professional meeting with a group of young people who provided their perspective about the topics at hand. As the meeting progressed, it was clear that the young people in the room were not encouraged to contribute to the conversation. As I perceived the situation, the young man sitting beside me slipped a piece of paper in front of me. Written on the paper was a question, asking if he could interject and confront the meeting about their exclusion as young people. I looked at the language that he intended to use and wrote in response, "Yes, but can you please tone down the language?" He looked at me and shook his head. I braced myself.

He found his opportunity and challenged the room about the presence of young people who were clearly not included in the conversation. The room fell silent. The energy dropped, and I sensed the forced discomfort amongst those present. I felt myself questioning my own intentions and actions. I wondered, who I was to ask someone else to water down their expression around what they felt needed to be said so that I would feel more comfortable with shaking the boat a little less? And who I was to position myself as a gatekeeper where this young person very clearly knew exactly what needed to happen to bring the space into higher alignment?

The deal with leadership is that once those we lead begin to find their feet, we need to get out of their way and learn how to help them do what they need to do. The span of a pendulum expands to include both wrapping others in cotton wool, leaving them to their own devices, and every space in between. Our ultimate task is to reinstate self-ownership, agency and sovereignty to each individual. Too many of us have not had a consistent experience of knowing what it is like to speak and act for ourselves, and this is an essential muscle to be built in shifting the trajectory of humanity. Vandana Shiva, an Indian scholar and activist, states that we do not need to empower women, as women already have power. We all have power, and we all need the support and opportunities that enable us to define and channel this power for ourselves.

For some time, I worked within an organization where it was regularly commended that we did not see a lot of the "high risk" behavior that other organizations saw in young people. One day, a young man came to meet me. As I casually greeted and welcomed him into the old inner-city townhouse in our office, he walked around and seemed a little confused, but was, however, also relaxed in his stance. I asked him if he was hungry or thirsty, invited him into the kitchen, opened the fridge door and suggested that I could make him a toasted sandwich. I asked him what he wanted to do, suggesting he could choose where we hung out or that we could go upstairs and hang out with others in my work team at their desks. After chatting with the others working in the building, we returned to the front room, which had the impression of a living area with lots of artwork and positive and colorful affirmations scattered around.

At this point, the young man shared with me, "there's something unusual about this place that I can't put my finger on." I enquired further. He stated, "Well, it doesn't feel like an office - it just feels like I've walked into someone's house and been told to make myself at home. It's cool... but it's weird." He continued to explain that, typically, his experience of visiting an office means walking into a formal building, pressing a buzzer, and having a conversation with a formally dressed person about who he is and why he was visiting. He would sit and wait, and he may be buzzed into a private room where a worker would meet him, and they would sit opposite one another at a table with pen and paper between them.

This young man's experience of meeting me told a very different story from its inception. It has long been said that we say to a room about who we are when we enter it, and the opposite is also true. The rooms that we enter tell us a lot about how they respond to, value, hold and meet the needs of those who visit or spend time in them. Every single element of who we are, the spaces we inhabit and produce, the language that we use, all serve the purpose of sending a message and vibration about who we are and how strongly our words and actions are aligned with what we hold as our truth. This space allowed this young man to trust my legitimacy in valuing his presence as a human.

Brene Brown states, "The middle is messy, but this is where the magic happens." My best example of this is best described by facilitating camps for young people. Day one would typically be characterized by nervousness, shyness and uncertainty. On day two, a lid would lift, which tended to bring upset, triggers and young people wanting to leave camp. Day three would bring group hugs, sadness and claims about how much they would miss each other. Despite the strongest skill set, few things prepare any of us for the messy middle. We learn through being in it.

In one camp, a visibly distressed young woman ran off at night. Three camp facilitators followed the young woman, who was found standing on a cliff edge. One facilitator gently approached and sat near the young woman, and started a conversation with her. The other facilitator and I stayed back a little, observing the situation. The facilitator, alongside me, began pacing nervously and asking me what he should "do." Should he try to bring the young person down? Should he go back to camp? I suggested that he do neither, and that he sit and be present.

He seemed perplexed and sat uncomfortably beside me. I assured him that I was well aware of the potential risk in the situation… and that the best thing that we could do at that moment was to sit at a distance and be present. To trust the space, to trust our fellow facilitator and to trust our young person. All was in order, and they both knew that we were nearby, supporting and strengthening them. In time, both came down from the cliff edge and we walked back to camp together. The young person knew what she needed; she had created the space for herself to process what had impacted her, and she knew that she was supported in doing this. The messy middle is what makes and, often, is what comes to define the best of us.

I was once asked to sit on an "Expert Panel" for what was seen as my innovative work with young people. I openly shared that I am not an expert in anything; I am merely prepared and committed to exploring things. If something works, I do it again, and if it doesn't, I'm prepared to move on. And so is the essence of the messy middle. It's the capacity to sit with what is and to navigate what is in front of us with the best of what we have available at the moment, and to bring the most humanity that we can to it.

I worked with a young man who wanted more than anything to meet and establish a relationship with his father. I found his father and spoke to him about meeting his teenage son and understanding his forming identity. The father decided that he would not like to meet his son. I sat with this information and wondered how to inform the young man, especially at a point where he was going through a particularly unsettling time. I was unsure whether the young man could hear what I had to share and navigate the potential impact of this.

During a meeting amidst a room of professionals and the young person himself, I was asked directly if I had contacted the young man's father. I looked directly at the young man, as I explained that I had made contact. I was asked to explain the outcome of my communication with him. As I explained that the father did not wish to meet his son, I felt appalled with myself and how this had been shared. The meeting progressed as though what I had just shared held no significant value, like something belonging in the middle section of a newspaper.

After the meeting, I braced myself and took a moment to speak to the young person alone. I took a deep breath and apologized for not being upfront with him about my communication with his father. I apologized for not trusting in his capacity to hold such valuable information about his own life. I also apologized for how it came out and the lack of care that was taken in this. He looked at me and said, "It's ok." I wondered how he could be okay with what could possibly best be described as him having learned to be alright with not expecting better from a system that had held him with such little care. I responded with, "It's not ok that this has happened this way. It's also ok to feel however you feel about this." It is not our responsibility to cushion the reality of anyone's life. Compassion instead asks that we sit with others in the space where there may be no real solution, and that we are in the reality of it together.

All of us are way-showers as much as we are space holders, and all else is a delivery method for this. "I couldn't hear the stories and do what you do" is a typical response to my work. I can't help but challenge this with, "How could I hear the stories and not do what I do?" We are not born ready for this, and there is no real preparation possible for a lot of the situations that we find ourselves inhabiting. We can only take what is in front of us, love it and do our best to weave magic in it. We are not and cannot be expected to be ultra-human. However, we can commit to being more attuned to what will bring a deeper experience of humanity and connection to the occasion. We are asked to continue to return to this truth and to again expand from this space. We are asked to trust our capacity to hold what is put in front of us, to become the bigger person and grow into the response that it demands of us.

I worked with foster caregivers who remortgaged their home to pay the legal fees to provide a home and family for five siblings until they reached adulthood. One of the caregivers had left her profession to assist the children in addressing their trauma. The story of these children was not only their stories; it was the story of generations of their ancestors, and these caregivers had stood up to change this trajectory. In walking alongside, holding and watching this story unfold, how could I do anything but spend a day on the stand in court, advocating for this story to continue to unfold as it was best served through these caregivers? Once we realize that our individual selves are both incredibly small, and also just as inherently powerful in the scheme of what humanity and life ask of us, we learn that we have the potential to create ripple effects that expand much further than we can begin to otherwise imagine.

I want to share one final story. In preparing a young person to undertake an important speaking piece for the launch of a government program, I asked her what she felt most passionate about sharing. The young woman shared with me the importance of young people having adults in their lives who hold higher expectations of them. She shared that one key reason she completed her secondary school education was that a particular teacher would call her each morning and insist that she got up for school. If she refused, the teacher would come to her house and demand that she got ready. This teacher's care and belief are what this young woman attributes to her choosing a very different trajectory in life.

On the day of our presentation, the young woman did not arrive. I became nervous as her phone continued to ring out. She eventually answered her phone as the presentation start time drew near. She had had a few hours of sleep and told me that she was too tired to attend, and she did not feel ready. I thought quickly. "How long will it take you to get ready? I asked. "About 10 or 15 minutes, why?" I looked at my watch. This may work. "I'm ordering a cab to bring you here. Text me when you're in the cab, I will call you and we will prepare. What do you need when you arrive? Coffee? I'll meet you at the cab with coffee and bring you in. You'll have a few minutes and have to walk straight in and present." I was surprised when she responded with, "Ok. I'm getting ready."

She arrived, walked straight in and up to the stage, and presented an incredibly powerful piece around our public service system's responsibility in holding higher expectations for young people from complex backgrounds. This message began a conversation through two major public sectors across the state at all levels, and it contributed significantly to the expansion and longevity of the program at hand. Further programs and resources were created to meet this critical gap for young people. Significant change can be easy. However, it demands that we hold people accountable for what they stand for, and it insists that they show up when it matters and the environment is ready for the real conversation to be held. It also asks the same of us.

The spaces that we hold as leaders are where humanity will be transformed. We are at a time where we cannot afford to minimize or see our role in any other way. We are being asked to bridge separation and use leadership as a vehicle to express, hold accountable and shift the trajectory, so that both enable us to bring more of ourselves to the forefront while encouraging others to do the same. We are asked to exist at a higher frequency, more sustainably and in ways that help us evolve beyond our current states of operation. We are asked to consider, "Is this good for me, others, society and the planet? And how do we use this to impact the greater good?" What is being asked of us is as complex as it is simple. We are being asked to be present, open, attuned and connected. And that we meet ourselves and one another over and over again.

"People don't mind being challenged to do better if they know the request is coming from a caring heart."

~ Ken Blanchard

CHAPTER EIGHT

Personal Leadership for a Sustainable Future

By Lillian Tahuri

Taking action and contributing to climate change action doesn't have to be on a large scale. Little acts of millions of people can make a huge impact. If everyone stopped using single-use plastic bags, that alone would have an enormous positive impact on the environment. Americans use 100 billion plastic bags a year, requiring 12 million barrels of oil to make. Over 100,000 marine animals are killed by plastic bags each year, and one in three turtles have been found with plastic in their stomachs. Some governments worldwide have halted the use of single-use plastic bags as an easy win toward sustainability. Plastic bags can also take 500 to 1000 years to decompose.

Consumers are more conscious of where their food is coming from and how it is grown. Demand for ethical and organic food has grown over the last decade. The expectation is growing for labels to include all ingredients and place of origin. Parents are now looking for organic and ethically grown food for their young families, and supermarkets have responded with shelves of products.

The amount of water used to make one t-shirt is enough for one person to consume for 2.5 years. Through recycling, small acts by individuals can slow the demand for new goods and impact how many resources are required.

Food waste is the second-largest source of methane pollution in our atmosphere. As an individual, you can choose to shop for what you actually need to limit food waste. You can move away from buying single-use plastic water bottles, and opt for a sustainable, reusable one. What we demand as a consumer is what drives demand. Demand sustainable, reusable and recyclable products, and repurpose to donate other goods you no longer need.

The world that we live in is in constant change, influenced by those in power, whether it is political or the power of money, and this has severely impacted our environment. International trade has opened up across the globe, where previously many countries had tightly managed the economic and social impact of imported and exported goods. Cheap clothes, cars, electrical goods and just about anything else that could fit on a ship started flowing into the country. Simultaneously, the mass production of food and farming keeps increasing as the international markets opened up.

Our lifestyle of fast food and cheap, convenient goods is in full flight. We are stripping Earth of its resources in the sea and on land. We have polluted the air that we breathe, the water that is essential for life, and the earth that we live on.

Science tells us that we must stop what we're doing and find more sustainable ways to live on this planet. The world is very slowly moving toward this direction with the signing of the Paris Agreement in 2016, which brought all signatory nations into a common cause to undertake efforts to combat climate change, adapt to its effects and support developing countries to do so as well. It is a global response to keep a global temperature below 2 degrees Celsius above pre-industrial levels.

Our country, New Zealand, is a signatory to the Paris Agreement. On our world scale, our impact on the environment is small, but there is much to do here. Our government has taken four years to declare a climate emergency due to the political party's positions.

It will take political leadership to make changes on a large scale. It is a transformational cultural change that will take years to develop. Corporations, large and small, that benefit from their current behaviors will use every effort to resist change. It's not going to be easy.

It will take personal leadership and ownership of our decisions to improve the environment. It is all the small decisions on whether we buy food in plastic, recycle our clothing, pass on household goods to others who need it and buy products that have a small environmental footprint to goods grown or manufactured locally.

It is up to us to ensure we have political and business leaders that subscribe to a sustainable future. Our votes count for the future we expect for ourselves and future generations. We all have the buying power to move the market toward products manufactured and grown sustainably.

Grandad's Orchard, Chickens and Sheep

We're off to see grandad on the short nine-kilometer journey that at a young age seems like an eternity. As we get closer to his home, we can see his tree-lined property coming into view. The trees are evergreen, close together, and form a solid barrier. As mum approaches the corner, she slows the car down and we try to peer through the wall of trees to get a glimpse of his house. We can't see through the trees, as usual, but that has never stopped us from trying.

Mum drives around the corner and we all look out for his old gray Morris Oxford, hoping to see it parked outside on the worn bridge in front of the garage door. This side of his property is lined with the same evergreen trees, heavy with branches and thick with leaves. This is interrupted by a small gate to enter the property and the garage door. The sight of grandad's car starts the wave of excitement that he is home. If it's not, it's anxiousness and hopes that it's in the garage and he is there. This scenario plays out for every visit.

Grandad was born in 1907, and during the first world war years, his mother struggled to raise him and his siblings on her own. She left three of them in an orphanage while his father was away on the western front. He never talked to us about those times; we were too young. We noticed how close he and his brothers were, and it was always a big occasion when they came together. They were all men of few words, warm, friendly hearts and they all wore hats.

Rushing into granddad's home was the storm before the calm. We would all rush in to see him, loud and hyped up, and he was calm and smiling. We would be all shy, quiet and polite through the cakes, biscuits and cordial. Once the news exchange had been completed for us kids, we would run out to see what was happening.

Grandad had paddocks with sheep in them. It never occurred to me that that was the meat we were actually eating when we were at his place. Let's not talk about the chickens running around with their heads cut off to traumatize young minds and become stories that last a lifetime. Every so often, the sheep were let into the property around his home. Their job was to mow the lawn, by eating it and then fertilizing it. The grass was always green and luscious.

First, we would check the hen house to see if there were any eggs to gather. Then, we'd check if the walnuts were drying in his second garage that he never seemed to use, and this included tasting them. Depending on the season, we would sit in his personal orchard and eat peaches, nectarines, oranges, apples, pears, grapes, plums and loquats. I especially liked the chestnut tree; I think we all did. We would get a pile of chestnuts and he would heat them for us and put loads of butter on them.

Our visit always included an inspection of his tree that grew both oranges and lemons. I don't know how many times they told us that grandad had grafted orange branches onto a lemon tree. It fascinated us, and we always asked.

By the time we had to leave, we had overindulged on fruit, and he was giving us brown paper bags full of fruits and walnuts. Grandad had far too big a harvest to keep all to himself, so he shared everything with all our relations. Many years later, a friend of mine told me they used to sneak into his property and raid his trees. I thought this was really interesting and had a good laugh. Grandad would tell us, with a smile on his face, that he saw the kids in the neighborhood come in and help themselves to the fruit. I guess it was his way of sharing, while pretending not to see or hear them.

Seafood, Vegetables, and Watercress

On my father's side of the family, my grandmother was born in 1905, and my grandfather in 1906. Unlike our mother's family, they are Maori and from different tribes here in New Zealand. For our entire lives, we have grown up and lived in two worlds. Back when our parents were married, it was frowned upon to marry someone of a different race, but here we are, the next generation of a mixed marriage.

119

I noticed back then, but took for granted that this side of our family talked about the moon, stars, the seasons, tides, timing and weather patterns. According to this knowledge, they would know when to go fishing, eeling, collect shellfish, plant crops and gather food. They also knew if certain trees were blooming early, whether it was time to gather certain seafood, and when it would be at its best harvesting time.

We also learned when it was time not to take shellfish and gather other food resources. Occasionally, a ban was put on certain resources so that it could replenish itself. Everyone in the community would hear by word of mouth not to touch certain resources until a ban was lifted. This was not a government ban, but a Maori cultural practice and management of resources that everyone followed, including non-Maori in our community.

There were and still are certain practices when taking food resources. These practices applied to everyone in the community. You never take more than you need for you and your family. You share what you have with other family and friends who cannot go out and get their own. We grew up with family members dropping off seafood and vegetables. In turn, our mother would share what she could with others.

Growing up at that time, it seemed everyone knew how to dive, fish, hunt, and garden. When we visited our grandmother's home, she would be cooking pots of food for the entire family. Our cousins would be smoking fish and eels in a make-shift smoker. The wider family would go out fishing and hunting together. The family planned to go out together according to the seasons, tides, and moon phases. It wasn't an over-managed process, but a casual conversation that people had with each other because everyone knew the cultural practices. These cultural practices spilled over into the non-Maori community and became widely adopted. They were known to guarantee success. It wasn't a big deal. It was just done and accepted by the community.

There is a lot to learn from Indigenous communities around the world about conservation, sustainable use and taking care of nature. Conservation of natural resources, caring for the forests, seas and waterways has been the lifeblood for these communities. Indigenous people have a direct relationship with nature; it is part of their cultural identity – look after nature and nature will provide. Maybe it is time for us as individuals to open doors for indigenous knowledge and practices to be introduced into our government and corporate approaches and taken seriously.

The Good Old Days: Lifestyle Blocks and Sustainable Living

My parents' and grandparents' generations lived an organic and sustainable lifestyle that many strive to achieve today. They were still cultivating food for themselves and their community, using resources around them sustainably, crafting, recycling and repurposing materials. The early conservationists' lifestyle was promoting, while being ridiculed by those in the modern world of convenience, the "use once and throw away" culture that was coming of age.

It is easy to look back and romanticize their lifestyle, but the sustainable lifestyle was how the generations lived before them. The world was before the information age, before inventions that have radically shifted our cultures. Each generation has lived through its own hardships. My parents, and, in particular, my grandparents, lived through two world wars that had social and economic impacts for generations. From what our mother tells us, times were hard throughout the war and post-war years, and they relied on animals for eggs and meat. Everyone kept gardens and had fruit trees. Nearly everyone had homemade or handed down clothes. Small town and rural communities were still using tank water from rain catchment, the garden compost took care of the food waste and shopping bags were made from paper bags and not plastic.

Although cars were big, slow and ran on petrol or diesel, there were fewer worldwide. As technology improved, so did the rate of extracting oils, minerals and other resources from the earth. Production of goods also increased. The population level rose and is still rising today, escalating demand for food, water and goods, and putting more pressure on the earth to provide for us all.

The natural and sustainable practices of the past were born out of need, scarcity, the economic times, and the lack of information and technology that we have today. The opportunity is now to take lessons from the past and to lead the way by bringing back practices that reduce our carbon emissions. It is time to influence local and central governments to create the laws and regulations that support these practices.

Made at Home

Home-cooked meals, bottling fruit, sewing, knitting, gardening, hunting and fishing were everyday activities for many households. If you couldn't do any of it yourself, you knew someone who could. Our mother was an all-rounder; she could do just about anything, and she passed her skills on to us.

Many of us had hand-me-down clothes, including our school uniforms. It was always an extra treat if you were given something brand new. Everything was used until it was worn out, or handed down to someone else if it was still good. This was just the way it was in our small, rural town. We were fortunate that our mother could sew because she would make us original and fashionable clothes if we were going somewhere, unlike some of our friends. It wasn't unusual back then for our mother's generation to undo a woolen garment to make something else. It seemed like they all had bits of wool and material ready and waiting for some unexpected event. They would also share what they had with each other, including lending their sewing machines.

Every season, the fruit and jam preserving would take place in our kitchen, and, for most of it, I avoided having to assist other than peeling peaches. Our cupboards were always filled with preserves, many of which were given away to others.

Home-cooked meals were made from scratch, salads didn't come in a bag, vegetables came out of the garden and were not prepared and ready to cook. Cakes, slices, scones and pavlova were all homemade and not sold by the thousands on supermarket shelves.

Food waste was sorted out from the rest of the household rubbish and put into make-shift compost bins that most gardeners seemed to have. Sometimes it was saved for pigs owned by friends or family members who would drop by regularly to collect the food waste.

Back then, it was common for neighbors to help each other and share what they had. The men would share lawnmowers, wheelbarrows and other tools. They would help each other cut hedges and clear properties. It wasn't uncommon to see the men in the neighborhood fixing each other's cars when required.

Many of our neighborhoods are no longer like this. However, is it now time for us to create spaces in our local communities to share, donate and swap goods and services?

From Childhood to Growing up Years

It was about this time that I heard people talking about vegetarians. For our mother's generation, not eating meat was a strange thing indeed. A small group of people did not want to participate in the changing world but wanted to keep the old ways, living off the land, not killing animals, and minimizing the impact they have on their environment.

People started talking about the impact of industrial waste in our local river, which included a meat processing plant, releasing effluent straight into the river on the outgoing tide. It was not uncommon for local governments to send untreated sewage out into the ocean, with much of it coming back up onto the beaches. The sound of small planes coming and going into the tiny airfield was regular background noise. They would load up on fertilizer and drop it across many of the farms without any thought of how that might impact the environment.

Family, friends and neighbors dropped by or stopped in the street to talk with each other. It was a great way of catching up on what was going on in the community. It was also one of the main sources of making complaints and stirring up trouble, as they were often described.

The tiny local paper came out three times a week with local information and stories. The letters to the editors seemed to come from those stirrers and troublemakers. Every so often, there would be a letter to the editor about the management of pollution in the river, and occasionally a short story about complaints to the local government authority.

In-depth information on any topic was limited to newspapers, the public radio, public television and libraries. Compared to the information age we live in today, our knowledge and experiences back then were minimal, shallow and in context to the environment we lived in.

In high school, social studies provided a wider view of world events from a social perspective depending on the teacher you had - some would only teach based on their limited experiences. In contrast, others had more knowledge and shared it freely.

Encyclopedia Britannica was the holy grail of information for all schools if you were fortunate enough to have a set. We had a set in our school library that sat waiting for the next group of students to refer to the same set of topics, as the curriculum didn't seem to move forward with the times. It was easy to spot the pages as they were well worn, and, in some cases, dog-eared while untouched volumes and pages still looked clean, straight, and new.

Becoming Woke

Woke is a term that has been described generally as being socially and politically awake or aware. It can also be used as a derogatory term to describe someone pretentious about being aware of social and political issues. Social issues are important to me and have been throughout my life. I see social and environmental issues as impacting each other; you cannot separate them.

I describe myself as the former in regard to environmental issues that impact the world we live in. In these early years, I became woke watching Dr. Seuss's *The Lorax* for the first time. Of course, I didn't know what woke was then. I just knew we needed to take care of the environment.

In these early years, I started taking notice of what was happening to the environment around us in our small town. If you raised your head above the crowd to speak on an issue, you were most likely going to be ridiculed.

Looking back, the lack of information was very narrow and localized. Everything printed was controlled by editors of newspapers, radio and television. It must have been hard for anyone to speak up on a particular issue and get a broad support base.

From the little knowledge I could gain in our community, it was the start of a journey to understanding the impact we have on the environment and what individuals can do about it and its consequences.

A Life of Convenience, Packaged and Ready to Go

The world was growing up fast and so was I. It was my turn to raise my two children, but in a very different world from my parents and grandparents. Many of us from our small rural town had moved to bigger cities for job opportunities. There were limited opportunities in our hometown, and, in many cases, it was a matter of waiting for someone to retire or die before a job opened up.

The cities were starting to expand with the influx of people from small towns or rural communities, which created many opportunities. Higher education was not required to get an outstanding job - there was a lot of on-the-job training and apprenticeships while working. It was an ideal way of having a job and becoming qualified at the same time.

Raising my family followed the same pattern as the generations before me, but that became increasingly difficult. In the early years, all meals were cooked at home, and there was time to have a small garden, sew and knit. Our neighbors were the same. We all knew each other. Our children played together in our homes, the park or on the streets.

Even though we were all following in the footsteps of the generations before us, the world was changing. We didn't have as many fruit trees. We didn't keep chickens or other animals on our city properties. To get ahead, many of us women were returning to the workforce to supplement the family income. Our children were being cared for by friends, neighbors, or in daycare and afterschool programs.

Take-out food shops became more popular; where once they were a treat, they soon became a once a week meal of convenience. American food giants like McDonald's and others were establishing themselves around the world with well-funded marketing campaigns.

Young working mothers moved away from reusable cloth diapers to the convenient disposable, synthetic and used only once. The impact of this one product alone was never considered from an environmental perspective. Supermarket chains started packaging convenient packs of meat, fish, fruits and vegetables. Boxes of easy to prepare meals, desserts and cakes could be taken off the shelf and whipped up in minutes.

As mothers' working hours increased, less time and energy was available for the lifestyle of our parents and grandparents. Bottling fruit, gardening, sewing and knitting were being replaced very quickly with products bought off the shelf. New products were continually coming out for our convenience. Microwaves to cook our food faster, video recorders to watch movies at home and numerous kitchen appliances from bread makers to air fryers.

The packaging alone for all food and household items was slipped into our way of living without a second thought. The fast-food products, with preservatives and other chemicals, quietly entered the economy and our bodies, unquestioned for many decades.

NGOs, Clothes Swaps, and Chickens

The world continues to change. Today, we are witnessing individuals to large corporations and governments taking action to protect the environment and build a sustainable future for all.

It was not so long ago when environmental activists were laughed at and jeered at for what was claimed to be hopeless causes that would never be achievable. While some are still called tree huggers, woke or referred to as wearing tinfoil hats, environmental activism has shifted toward the mainstream.

There is now a proliferation of environmental protection organizations worldwide, like The Sierra Club, Environmental Defense Fund, Greenpeace, The Nature Conservancy, World Wide Fund for Nature, Rainforest Action Network and Sea Shepherd Conservation Society - the list goes on.

There are large international organizations to small local community groups that work toward improving a wide range of environmental issues, including air quality, cleaner water, land use, waste, pollution, beach clean-ups and climate change.

On the other side are the even larger corporations and countries that rely on deforestation, fossil fuels, over-fishing and farming, to release pollution into the environment, including carbon emissions. These power brokers have an international reach and political base to ensure that they can continue their harmful practices for profit and minimize or slow down progress for a sustainable future. Large corporations and countries have the resources to infiltrate and undermine NGOs that are making a difference. For them, it is about protecting profits and keeping their power base.

Some years ago, I took a few weeks out of my life to volunteer for a non-government organization and joined a team of international activists. I discovered that the organization and individuals were targeted, and organized tactics were used regularly to undermine progress. International media campaigns were launched against the NGO, affiliated individuals and property were surveilled, individuals were planted on the inside, and family members were threatened. Some of the international activists stayed out of sight because they were fearful for their families.

During this time, I experienced many ordinary people dropping off donations, goods, food and words of support for the NGO. These people were from all walks of life, young and old. Today, awareness and information on environmental issues are easily accessible. People can find out information themselves; they don't need to wait for news items or search for information at a library.

I have been part of women's groups that hold clothes swaps. People bring good quality clothing at clothes swaps that they no longer use and swap them for items someone else has brought. Leftover clothes are then given to charity shops. It has been estimated that wearing our clothes for an extra nine months reduces clothing's carbon, water, and waste footprint by around 20-30%. Synthetic fabrics like polyester, spandex, and nylon take anywhere between 20 to 200 years to decompose.

Women are now swapping jewelry among themselves. Jewelry that was once treasured but no longer worn is now being rehomed. Old costume jewelry is being swapped. Each piece is given a second, and sometimes third, chance at life with someone who wants it, instead of sitting in a box hidden away for a year or more. Secondhand designer clothes shops are popping up everywhere, selling on consignment. There are now secondhand clothes shops for all budgets.

There are now chickens in urban areas supplying city dwellers with fresh eggs every day. I have four friends who keep chickens in their backyards, free-range and well-fed- just like my grandfather. Urban fruit and vegetable gardens are flourishing as people want to grow their own food. Community gardens are being established where the neighborhood comes together to grow their own vegetables, fruits and herbs. Supermarkets have designated special shelves just for organic food.

The notion of sharing has taken a modern twist, thanks to current technology and entrepreneurs: Airbnb, where people can rent out their homes or rooms to anyone; Uber, the car rideshare company; community electric bikes, scooters, toy libraries, tool and appliance share companies.

We live in the information age; we have information at our fingertips. We can communicate with anyone in the world instantly if they have internet access. The Digital 2020 July Global Snapshot published on the 21st July 2020 on the use of social media tells us that "4.57 billion people around the world now use the internet. Of those users, 346 million new users have come online within the last 12 months. There are 5.15 billion unique mobile users across the world."

We can influence change from our phones, tablets and computers through our social media accounts, reaching millions of individuals directly anywhere in the world.

The circle of life is slowing, taking us back to a more sustainable way of living, but this time with the assistance of technological and biological advances. We all know the science, and it is time to take personal leadership for a sustainable future for ourselves and future generations. We also know how to return our planet to what it was; we have been told by numerous scientists and nature adventurist, Sir David Attenborough. It is up to us, individuals, to make the changes, and to influence politicians and powerbrokers. If we listen to the science and take action, we will see the fish stocks in the oceans increase, the reforestation on the planet and improved water quality.

Hopefully, one day soon, we will start seeing suburban streets covered in community gardens and fruit trees, and perhaps a field dedicated to free-range chickens. Imagine streets with no cars, safe for walking and rideshare bicycles, skateboards, wheelchairs and e-scooters. I can see the public transport system becoming an ethical and cool way for regular commuters across large cities.

"Papatuanuku, our earth mother, will continue with or without us. It is up to us."

"If your actions inspire others to dream more, learn more, do more and become more, you are a leader."

~ John Quincy Adams

CHAPTER NINE

Oneness in Leadership

By Mariese B. Vacalares

I Am pieces of a puzzle flowing in harmony.
We are pieces of the puzzle, coming together as One.
We complete each other and find strength in our unity.
Together. we can make the world a better place.

I believe I am showing up here to connect with you as an act of oneness, an act in synchronicity.

I come to disrupt some leadership concepts for this new era. Most predominantly in the year 2020, a new paradigm of leadership strongly emerged. I may call it the Spirit of Oneness. It lives and comes alive in every one of us when we accept and allow it as the guiding force to motivate us into personal integration of our mind, body and spirit, of our lower and higher selves, an integration of our human and divine natures. This propels and leads us to collaborate with others to build harmonious relationships and empower us to transform societies and communities.

The year 2020 started with me excitedly buying a new laptop solely to write a book. It's been about a decade since I first wanted to write some books, but despite connecting with coaches and mentors, certain circumstances prevented me from writing.

The days dragged, and then, the bomb was dropped. The pandemic hit worldwide and I eventually entered lockdown at home with my parents. A few days after, I had a physical attack that compelled me to call a healer and find some natural remedies, rather than going to the hospital. This marks the zone where something out there is not normal, and I had to learn to adapt fast.

The turn of events was something I was not prepared for, but for some reason, this was something I had longed for: to keep still, take hold of the moment, shut out all distractions, focus, reach for the stars and arrive at a destination.

At the time of this writing, I am in the middle of the second wave of this pandemic in 2020, still in lockdown at home for months and forced to resolve my issues. Yet the world made a 360-degree turn, and what used to be impossible now seems to be possible. While the rest of the world has been disempowered, some of us are empowered to do things we have never done before: expanding our consciousness, mindsets, heartsets, soulsets and skill sets.

While some of our family businesses closed down, I was learning to live by myself with just my aging parents, doing household chores and cooking daily as a home-based chef. It was difficult when some of our househelp who got sick went home and the other got pregnant. Businesses continued and flourished online so that zoom meetings, dressed in suits or blazers with shorts and sandals or barefoot, became frequent and fashionable in this new normal.

I was connecting with the most prominent coaches and mentors online. It was inspiring that they wanted to serve more in these unprecedented times. I salute the true leaders, mentors, coaches and influencers who stood strong while the rest of the world tumbled down. More and more, though, I was losing grip of my reality while growing in spirit and trying to hold on for dear life and God, my Creator, despite whatever drama and destiny the world has been undergoing in these troubled times. It was exhilarating to think that these hardships pushed us to our limits, causing us to connect with our higher selves for guidance, protection and divine help and intervention. S.O.S. And then they came. I felt angels and archangels surrounding me as I continued to call on them with my prayers and daily rosary.

Then, someone posted a lovely picture of her 62nd birthday celebration in our Facebook group. It was the fantastic artist and amazing coach, Gabriela Delgadillo, who received 10,000 greetings on her recent birthday. She posted such remarkable images and replies that I connected on her group chats and pages for healing, business and even this book-writing breakthrough, linking with the amazing John Spender, publisher of the *A Journey of Riches* series. The rest is history. This is the power of her leadership, collaboration, love and service.

Given this challenge and opportunity to write and crack the code, I began to write about my journey through the years dealing with my issues on healing, spirituality and entrepreneurship. Then, I realized that Oneness is a new paradigm of leadership, and it could be applied for an individual person, for a group or organization or for positive changes or transformation of a group or community. How I came to discover this truth is the culmination of a long journey that started in my childhood.

It was one of those lovely, sunny days perfectly etched in my childhood memory, a day of great revelation as it holds a vision of my dreams of what I wanted to be when I grow up. It's a wonder to recall the following scenario when I was in primary school.

The road up the hill was a little steep. I was looking down on my two little feet carrying me to my school about 400 meters away from home, wondering as I groped for words to describe how I wanted to be when I grew up. When I saw two words, my little brain lighted up. I wanted to be a scientist and a businessman.

Now, I thought these were two big words for an eleven-year-old. What would it be like to be a scientist and a businessman? How did I come up with these ideas? Perhaps it runs in the family. Yes, my grandma, Fortunata, was an extraordinary entrepreneur of sorts, and so is my mom, Vilma, a pioneering chemistry teacher and pharmacist by profession, who operated her own pharmacy and grocery store. My dad, Salvador, is a physics enthusiast, a self-taught mechanical-engineer-turned-businessman who invented his own machines. My sister Sarah, Uncle Rito and other relatives were medical doctors.

At such a young age, it was strange to feel that I didn't belong here - like I was *in* the world, but not *with* the world. I would look up to the skies for answers.

In high school, at barely 14 years old, I was in the library reading about stories on psychic surgery and books like *The Magicians of God: The Amazing Stories of Philippine Faith Healers* by Jaime Licauco, or winning interschool science projects on Pyramid Energy and passing my research paper requirement by writing on the subject of hypnosis. I was on my way to becoming a scientist.

Moving on from high school to college, my life continued in being the observer. I wasn't talking much through those years, not going out often with others, until such time when I was in my fourth year of college and I started to meet up with people in a few school organizations and the campus church choir.

Fresh from graduating college with a Bachelor of Science degree in Biological Sciences as my pre-medical course at the University of the Philippines, I created a movement in my hometown called OPCYM (Opol Christian Youth Movement), patterned after my university organization called UPCYM, just one of the few organizations I'd joined. I was also involved with the organization for biologists, UPECS (UP Ecological Society) and the campus church choir, from which I patterned my efforts to lead my church choir at home. As I gathered my elementary schoolmates and friends for this Christian youth movement, moving around town creating events and God-centered activities, I learned of the intricacies of religion and spirituality, of the pitfalls of leadership and human relationships and of oneness and diversity.

His Holiness the Dalai Lama, who is awakening people to the oneness of humanity, said, "When we're two or three years old, we don't care if other children's families follow this or that religion, or belong to this or that race, so long as they smile and play happily with us. From this point of view, young children are aware of the oneness of humanity. However, at school, we learn to identify differences between us, distinctions only of secondary value. Fundamentally, we're all the same in being human."

Oneness is defined in different aspects: unity, cooperation, harmony, peace, alignment, integration of mind, body and spirit; a space where there is agreement, support, teamwork, collaboration, trust, wholeness and like-mindedness.

My first encounter with the principle of oneness was my early experience with martial arts right after college, when I learned the Korean martial arts called Won Hwa Do, the Way of Harmony. The opposing principles of yin and yang are united in harmony in a circular motion. I learned the original martial arts' value as developed by the monks, a sacred and secret art later commercialized by celebrities. I also learned, here, the value of horizontal and vertical relationships.

My next encounter with the value and philosophy of oneness was my lesson when I joined the Art of Living Foundation, where one connects with the higher self and develops from being Nobody to being Somebody, then becoming Everybody.

To quote the founder of the Art of Living Foundation, His Holiness Sri Sri Ravi Shankar, in his address during the Global Oneness Summit in 2012.

"The God particle is discovered and the Oneness of the Universe is established by science. It authenticates what the relishes of ancient times said that the universe is made up of one consciousness. Everything is a play and display of one consciousness. There is no doubt that the universe is made up of one thing and we are part of that One. It's time to celebrate that oneness, spiritually and scientifically. There's a great advantage in recognizing this oneness and we start recognizing the diversity as well, and we start celebrating the diversity. Our diversity, our differences, can no longer be a point of contention or conflict. The new Awakening will start happening in every individual. Then, we start valuing our life more. When we value our life, we will value every other life on this planet. It's time we realize the Oneness of the Universe, Oneness of the human race, Oneness of all life. We need to create a sense of Belongingness with people of all religions, communities, races and nationalities. We are part of that One Universal Spirit. We are part of One Global Family. This will lead to a violence-free, stress-free society. Uncertainties, fears and hatred will disappear. There will be more love and compassion between people and communities. Where there is peace, there is prosperity. So, we can only see advantages when we recognize we are all One."

Here is where I also first learned yoga in the flesh, not from videos or books. Yoga taught me the integration of the mind, body and spirit into one enlightened whole being. My longer years as a student pursuing a bachelor's degree in biological sciences in college, and proceeding to a medical course but dropping out twice, then later finishing a master's course in human resource development, plus attending all kinds of seminars and workshops—all of these made me use my mind more often. I needed more balance with my heart, body and spirit. Yoga's integrative flow of movement helped me to do just that. Later, I was able to get a certification as a yoga teacher and work on it as an integrative tool for oneness. I later developed a lifestyle movement I call *Kai'yah* which I use as a transformational tool in my self-help programs.

Let me show you how I developed a kind of spirituality grown uniquely from my own circumstances. I was in medical school in my early twenties when I first got hold of a book entitled *The Lost Years of Jesus* from the nearest bookstore, followed by a four-book series on *The Lost Teachings of Jesus*. These were new and quite strange to me as they unraveled the lost years and teachings of Jesus revealed in the *Holy Bible*. Authored by the astonishing and remarkable couple, Mark and Elizabeth Prophet, they presented the story of Jesus as I have never seen before in any other sources publicly available. They taught about the missing texts on karma and reincarnation. They provided the missing links to the mysteries of the knowledge of our true identity and the power of our own inner Christ. They were able to recapture the heart of Jesus's message, that, just like Him, we can reconnect with our divine source to realize our full potential.

They told stories of saints and mystics who accomplished the goal of self-transcendence and gained immortality. They became the messengers of the Ascended Masters whose messages gather momentum to help liberate humanity to this day.

In *Unveiled Mysteries,* Ascended Master Godfre Ray King describes an Ascended Master as "an individual who by Self-Conscious effort has generated enough Love and Power within himself to snap the chains of all human limitation, and so he stands, free and worthy, to be trusted with the use of forces beyond those of human experience. He feels himself the Oneness of Omnipresent God-Life. Hence, all forces and things obey his command because he is a Self-Conscious Being of Free Will, controlling all by the manipulation of the Light within Himself."

As Mark Prophet became the Ascended Master Lanello in the 1970s, his wife, Elizabeth Prophet, continued to lead in the community they'd created at the Royal Teton Ranch in Montana, U.S.A. Their messages caught fire in the spiritual communities throughout the world. After she left, the latest Dispensation of the Messengers, Carolyn and Monroe Shearer, were announced. They now lead the *Temple of the Presence* located in the heart of Tucson, Arizona.

The Messengers taught about "Oneness with the Christ Presence, the I AM Presence, the Divine Self or Higher Self. As a leader you need to strengthen the presence of the inner Christ, the I Am Presence, putting on the garment of Virtuousness, the Christ consciousness in yourself, your family, your business and other endeavors. You need to internalize the Truth of your Divine Identity. Oneness with the Mighty I AM Presence in your Life is the Victory, that you are the One, moving forward to gain your victory ultimately. Your I AM Presence, or Divine Self, wants to participate in your life, so you do not just rely on your human consciousness or the mass consciousness. You have the opportunity to stand in your own light, your own victory. Thus, you would have fulfilled your destiny in this life."

It took me decades to understand and accept the teachings of the Ascended Masters, the immortal leaders like Jesus, Mother Mary, St. Germain, St. Francis or Kuthumi, St. Thomas More or El Morya, the Archangels, even the Buddha, Kuan Yin and Lord Krishna. I scouted around for the Ultimate Truth, comparing groups who study the same or different kinds of teachings.

One lesson I remembered from a master, Dr. Murdo MacDonald-Bayne, author of *Beyond the Himalayas,* was to "Let the Truth unfold without suggestions from outside; and you must not come to a conclusion, for this closes the avenue to Truth."

There was a recent significant event in my life that I could not forget when I visited the Temple of the Presence in Tucson, Arizona, with my parents and some friends in June 2016. When we arrived, the day's lecture was already unfolding. We were escorted at the sala by the hall outside the conference room where a television monitor showed the Messenger Carolyn Shearer presenting a live dictation by Ascended Master Godfre Ray King, formerly the embodiment of General George Washington. His message took me by surprise when he said, "You are commanded to fulfill your destiny!" My jaw dropped, and my hairs stood on end with goosebumps as I heard those piercing words. Recognizing that the message was from the former General George Washington, I felt I could stand at attention with a command from the general himself. I thought, *Wow, that's an order!* The short, but sharp soul-stirring message, now still ringing in my ears, was delivered just in time when we were properly seated outside of the prayer room where the rest of the congregation was gathered. Talk about destiny!

I gathered from these spiritual teachings that a person has a Higher Self or Divine Self. But many are not aware of the truth of one's own true nature, one's own divine heritage. In a book by Leona Lal-Singh, *Priests of the Order of Melchizedek*, Jesus revealed that humanity's greatest sin is ignorance of our true creative nature and our divine sonship with the infinite eternal life. This ignorance makes one see himself as separate from his Creator and disconnected from everyone else.

I used to be so sickly as a child that, at seven years old, I was already hospitalized for anemia. I always had coughs and colds, and it was only during my college days that I learned from Dr. Linus Pauling to heal myself with a mega-dose of Vitamin C.

Through the years, I learned to heal myself, not with drugs, but with natural alternative ways.

Fast forward to 2020. These unprecedented times caused me to hit rock bottom. One night, a few days after our neighborhood went into lockdown, I felt numb on my left side – my arm, my hand, the left side of my head. I went into emergency mode, thinking of all possibilities and what kind of illness it could be. It was almost midnight when I instinctively messaged my theta healer and teacher, Dr. Sanaiyah Gurnamal, for a healing session, which we scheduled for early the next day. I was advised to visit the hospital, but it wasn't what I wanted to do at midnight. I'd rather buy herbal medicines from Dr. Ed Wahiman than expose myself to the hospital. My unbalanced diet, along with the fear and the stress, knocked me down, but thanks to theta healing with my teacher and the herbal medicines, I quickly got help to balance my energies. I needed to believe in somebody and something to bring me into my own healing. But then I became aware of how my thoughts, my feelings and my beliefs could affect me, physically.

One time, while attending a seminar, a question was raised and I became aware of different parts of me responding differently to the question. I raised my hand to answer yes to the problem, but my mind seemed to disagree. Still, I felt indifferent and I believed the question didn't have to be answered by a yes or a no. A sense of disconnection and separation was what I felt in many ways.

Many times I felt there's something disconnected or in disagreement within me. I became aware of the inner resistance, the hard-headedness, the rebellious spirit from within that kept me separated and disconnected from my own inner and higher self.

After learning and getting certified as a theta healer, I asked my teacher about it. We did a session on this concern and I related that, by some semblance of synchronicity, I received some messages the day before we did the theta healing session. The answer to the issue was revealed in that angelic message - the lesson on the integration of the mind, heart, body, and spirit.

I tried it by heart to develop integration within myself through yoga and become attuned to the whole. I was listening to that still small voice during moments in silence or meditation. That at-one-ment with the spirit is the ultimate goal for Oneness. To take your growth to a higher level, you need to enter into oneness with God and oneness with all life.

Relying on human consciousness may not bring you the best of the ideals, but working with your divine consciousness leads only to perfection. Personal integration can be enhanced with practicing yoga and having a spiritual understanding of and a deep connection with your own Higher Self, your Divine Self.

After dropping out of medical school, I looked forward to shifting to alternative or complementary medicine, but I coursed through life distracted by so many shiny objects and getting exposed to many civic groups and business organizations. Sometime in 2004, I attended an international convention for the Anthroposophical Society, founded by German philosopher Rudolph Steiner, here in Cagayan de Oro City with about 300 participants from around the world—medical doctors, nurses, therapists, educators, nuns, pharmacists and other health associates.

In this 5-day live-in seminar, I learned that the principles of science and spirituality are smoothly combined, and that spirituality is much more of a science than just philosophy. We talked about chemistry and the elements—air, fire, water, earth, ether—which are all found in our bodies. It was interesting to discuss with medical doctors how silicon is a potent element in many chemical processes of creation. It was fun and enthralling to do our early morning exercises with an expressive movement art called *Eurythmy*, wherein every syllable uttered has a vibration with the corresponding movement, likened to that of an angel in the act of creation.

My young entrepreneurial mind and enterprising spirit started as early as ten years old, when I was selling candy to my classmates in elementary school. My mom used to operate a pharmacy and grocery with my grandma in their general merchandise store. I would stand on my toes and reach for the candy jars, counting them on the glass countertop above my head and deciding how many pieces I would take to school. I always felt elated when I could sell those candies and stuff to my schoolmates. Even in high school or college, I still had the itch to sell sundry things to everyone: clothing, jewelry, belts and bags, makeup, even subliminal and kiddy books and tapes. I would ask my cousin to tag along with me as we went around the neighborhood carrying the goods on my bicycle basket. I was later exposed to all kinds of businesses.

Then, something happened while I stayed at home after dropping out of medical school. A young man approached my father while doing business at his automobile shop. He was a member of the Unification Movement, The Holy Spirit Association for the Unification of World Christianity, founded by the Korean spiritual leader, the Reverend Sun Myung Moon. He was going to teach martial arts, Won Hwa Do, at our local community school and my father invited me to join them. After a series of sessions with the instructor, I was asked to help teach the younger kids.

Then, school was closed for summer and I invited students interested in working for a summer job at the beach property that my grandma used to own. By April, I had five kids, ages 11 to 13, working with me, cleaning the grassy portion of the beach area that was still undeveloped. Between work and play, we managed to do a few martial arts sessions by the beach with the soft wind blowing and the waves splashing by the shoreline, usually late afternoon before sundown. After some commands, they would playfully say, "Yes, master." It was a wonderful experience with these kids working, playing and studying martial arts. On consecutive early mornings, I would find them waiting for me at home downstairs so we could drive together to work at the beach.

It was my brainchild to develop the beach and put up umbrella-type huts along the shoreline. Without the knowledge of my father, who had gone abroad to the U.S., we managed to do some carpentry work with another adult student who joined us and carried on with the project, along with my mom's help and support. I drove my grandma's jeep with the trailer, and we carried some bamboos or lumber from the mountains. Soon, we were able to raise some wooden umbrella huts. It was almost June and summer was out. I had to say goodbye to my little workers. Then, before classes resumed for the next semester, I had to look for real carpenters to finish the project of putting up more umbrella huts by the beach. Years passed and these kids grew up to be businessmen, an accountant, a manager and career people, while the beach grew to be a go-to place for beach enthusiasts.

You can be victorious in your personal, organizational or community life when you're aligned with your Higher Self, bringing your highest ideals to share with the family, co-workers, teammates or partners and exhibiting, love, joy, peace, patience, kindness, goodness, faithfulness, gentleness, self-control…the fruits of the Spirit.

Then, I had another surreal experience combining my journey of healing, spirituality, entrepreneurship and leadership. One time, I was forced to find a doctor I thought could help me after being diagnosed with an illness. I was trying to chase down Dr. Romy Paredes, who I learned was supposed to conduct a seminar here. I went to this remote address, a long trip by bus, then by taxi. I arrived at a very remote village far from the hustle and bustle of the city, amidst the lush greeneries surrounding the fields at the widely developed *Enchanted Farm* of the Gawad Kalinga Village in Bulacan, Philippines.

I was standing by the roadside that sunny afternoon when suddenly and unexpectedly, a big white horse-driven carriage passed by me like a dream, and lo and behold, it was the popular founder of Gawad Kalinga himself, Mr. Tony Meloto, who was riding in the carriage. I could not believe what I saw, for I was not expecting to be transported to this village in so quick a time without warning.

On the first day of my five-day stay at the *Oasis Wellness Center,* located in the middle of the ten-hectare Gawad Kalinga Village, there were 15 staff members, mostly nurses and therapists working at the center. I happened to be the only client gracing the center with its unique spa and healing services. I later met Mr. Pi Villaraza, founder of Inner Dance, who accommodated me with a few healing sessions.

On the fourth day, the staff and I tried to visit some areas within the farm where the animals were housed and fed. Then, out of the blue, the white horse-driven carriage came again by the road with Mr. Meloto. To my surprise, he asked me to step up and join the ride with him to my destination. I felt this incident was symbolic of something. We even went to his house afterwards, and visited the Gawad Kalinga souvenir shop with their products like *Human Heart Nature* at the village's frontage near the residential housing projects up ahead. The visit, educational tour, healing experience and dreamy white horse-driven carriage ride with Tony Meloto was an inspiring and enlightening experience. I'd had an earlier vision similar to these, so it was no coincidence that I was able to meet him and see first-hand his active leadership for community development and social entrepreneurship for the Gawad Kalinga Community Development Foundation.

According to Google, answering the question of leadership may not be easy, considering that there are more than 30,000 definitions alone in the academe. Here are three focus areas of leadership that are commonly referred to, and which I associate with the areas of leadership development in correlation to Oneness:

a) Leading self: individual, leader = integration of the aspects of Self

b) Leading others: people, teams = collaboration with other Selves

c) Leading change: strategy and innovation, vision = transformation with Self, other Selves and their Environments

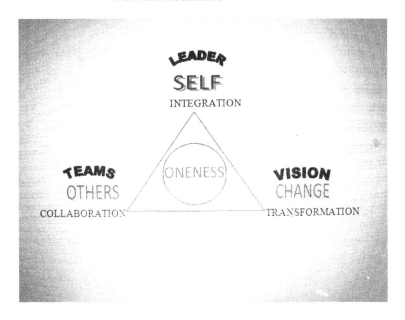

Figure 1. Illustration on Oneness

(This figure illustrates the correlation of Oneness in leading the Self, leading Others, and in leading Change.)

Oneness as a new paradigm of leadership starts with the integration of the whole person's being—his human and Divine natures aligned and connected. Once an individual is truly integrated, the genius, the leader, the master, the god from within emerges. He becomes a potential leader, able, willing and powerful enough to lead himself and others, and create positive changes in himself or in society. I believe it makes an ideal blueprint for a leader to mold into, and in this new era of the new normal, a new role model is emerging.

In many instances people feel like victims of their own circumstances, feeling not enough or unworthy, looking down on themselves and their human frailties. But if they make a conscious shift of identifying with the perfection of their Divine Selves, I see this as a remedy for many ailments in business and society.

For want of a new term, I would like to refer to this new leader as a Master Leader or a Neogenre, the Neoman, the Model Leader or simply The One—enlightened, awakened, aligned and attuned to his Higher Self. We would like to see this kind of leader occupying all positions in everyone's active lives: in the family, in business, in organizations, in the community.

I envision creating a program for a new paradigm of leadership with a Oneness Leadership Blueprint that includes a human software called the *Perfect Codes,* designed for what I call *biodynamic programming* on human DNA for the mindset, heartset, soulset, and skill set for the emerging Golden Age. Nothing is impossible with the many advances in science.

Leadership can guide others without force into a direction that leaves them still feeling empowered and accomplished.

Successful leadership is about making others better and making it last.

I have experienced different kinds of businesses, and recently discovered business growth and scalability through coaching. I was a seminar junky. I've taken seminars here and there, but I still felt a void, a disconnection, until I found the remedy or solution.

Tony Robbins and Dean Graziosi taught of new ways to ride the wave of adversity through creativity, using the Knowledge Industry as the new normal in this pandemic. Tony said, "I believe the quality of your life comes down to your level of leadership. It's the most important skill any human can master. A true leader inspires themselves and others to do, be, give and become more than they ever thought possible."

There are systems and strategies to develop a culture for extraordinary results, starting with building responsive relationships, a resourceful and productive state of energy with the team, unconditional commitment and performance beyond reason producing extraordinary results.

My business mentor on performance acceleration Rajiv Talreja said, "Now, I have evidence to prove that when you do the right things for the right reasons, the universe conspires in mysterious ways and gives you way more than what you can dream, anticipate or wildly imagine.

There's an energy of synchronicity when you tap into the Oneness.

Even Mahatma Gandhi said, "I suppose leadership at one time meant muscles; but today it means getting along with people."

Collaborative leadership shares control and handles conflicts in a constructive manner, while investing time to build relationships.

After my recent online encounter with two of the most creative people I found on the internet, I started to envision a business called Golden Gates Academy. It was like Saint Peter, the guardian of the gates of Heaven, tried to reach out to earth's people with two of his namesakes, Pedro Adao and Pete Vargas. These two coaches were some of the godliest people I've seen online. They both created an event called the Love, Serve, Grow Challenge last February 2020, just a few days before the pandemic hit worldwide. They later led me to tie up with Dean Graziosi and Tony Robbins in more online programs where I met our excellent coach, Gabriela Delgadillo.

There are several programs I'm developing as a response to the need for Oneness. Aside from the Golden Gates Academy where continuing education is the aim for everyone, there's the Tree of Life Foundation for counseling and therapy for the sick, displaced, elderly, disabled or differently-abled. A movement I call KAYA Centers (Kaya means empowered) will be established in strategic locations where specific groups, organizations, companies and agencies unite and share blessings, responsibilities, resources, skills, expertise and technology. Here is where Oneness and Best Practices are applied.

I look forward to creating a space of Oneness and inviting everyone to share this space as One Family.

A life worth living is when you're fully merged and aligned with God in Divine Oneness. That God is always with you, within you and all around you.

Oneness is living in peace, love, harmony, and cooperation within yourself and among all life—human, animal, and nature. This is the reality when you raise your frequency and vibration and expand your consciousness to a Higher Dimension heading into the Great Shift, the Ascension or the emerging Golden Age.

"A leader is one who knows the way, goes the way and shows the way."

~ John C. Maxwell

CHAPTER TEN

The New Business Value Proposition – People

By Russell Futcher

Leadership – "One of the most observed and least understood
phenomena on earth."
~ James Burns.

M any employees in organizations, today, are dissatisfied
with their jobs, feeling economically trapped, angry,
frustrated and unable to better their situation. The
brave move on; they are the risk-takers, and they find a way to do
better. But many remain trapped. What's going on? What are the
causes behind poor management and unhappy employees, and
when did it all begin?

The cause of this dissatisfaction may stretch back to the early
1880s and the Industrial Revolution, where cotton mills enforced a
type of control we know today as the Traditional Management
Model, also called the command and control structure — a term
referring to keeping subordinates in line. This management
approach, based on the hierarchical, and often brutal, British
military and naval traditions, typically involved the development
and implementation of strict rules of acceptable and unacceptable
behavior with harsh consequences for breaking the rules. The
Traditional approach underwent a refinement in the 1920s and
another after WWII, bringing about the management model that
dominates many of today's organizations.

Having gone virtually unchanged for almost 100 years, this model is typically structured like this: A senior executive or board holds all the power; they are in command and use their power and influence to lead. They appear at the top of the organization chart. Below them are senior managers, then middle managers, with employees at the bottom. We call this an organizational hierarchy.

According to author and organizational development expert, Peter Block, Traditional-style leaders are the senior managers who command respect through seniority and years of service, often viewed as tyrannical and intimidating. Their job is to plan, organize employees, direct and control. They set expectations for the employees below them who need to meet certain goals, but the manager receives the reward for achieving those goals. These managers also tend to experience a frequent turnover of employees.

New ideas from employees are not always welcomed; the managers see themselves as the source of all new business and ways of working. They can be blind to work and employment issues, and slow to react to change. Regrettably, the employees have learned that the way their managers act is what the path to success looks like, so they model it.

> Under Traditional models, "consistency and control were achieved through coercion and dominance. Organizations were set up as pyramids where power was distributed linearly from a small, select number of people at the top who controlled the majority of people positioned at the bottom. This top-down style of leadership was inherently hierarchical. Each leader was vested power and authority over those below them. These leaders often ruled with compulsion, force, control, secrecy, and—when necessary— physical, psychological, and/or economic violence. Thus, the tenets of Traditional leadership as we know it were established." Peter Block, Author and organizational development expert.

The Traditional management model is not about to disappear anytime soon, despite being plagued by employees who are dissatisfied with their jobs and unhappy with management, who provide little or no support and motivation. In many cases, managers still simply see their employees as units of labor, easily replaceable and not worth investing in. These organizations are also inferior at training their mid-level managers, preferring instead to invest in leadership training for senior executives.

Aside from today's organizations, we still see the Traditional model in use today, in strict hierarchical organizations such as the military and police. As a management model in these types of professions, it has proven to be enormously successful, contributing substantially to global economic growth and the employment of millions. Just like its origins, it is good at making profits, but this has come at a high cost. The Traditional model vests a lot of power in individual managers, allowing them to impose their own form of control, rules and regulations, just as long as they achieve business goals imposed on them from above. If not kept in check, this power can lead to abuse. Following is a modern-day example:

I was asked to do what I considered was a very tough assignment by the Chairman of a large Insurance Group for whom I had previously worked. I only accepted the job out of respect for the man concerned. His problem was that a well-known IT consulting firm with a notorious reputation for completely taking over and being difficult to move on had seized control of his IT Department. The consulting firm had been appointed by his European head office to develop new IT systems in Australia. The firm was also costing him a small fortune, and there was an increasing litany of problems occurring with a growing chorus of employee complaints. My brief was to find out what was going on, remove the consultants, fix the issues and restore service.

The day I arrived, I did so unannounced. As I was walking down a corridor looking for the office of the head of the consultancy, I overheard a voice say something like, "Run faster this time." With that, a banana peel came flying out of an office doorway into the corridor. This was followed by a distressed-looking young lady who quickly grabbed it and ran back into the doorway. I stood in amazement, then the whole scenario repeated itself, except this time with an instruction to "Do it faster."

Again, the banana peel came flying through the doorway, followed by the young lady chasing after it. I stood and waited to see how long this would go on. The whole scenario happened one more time, except this time I yelled out, "I'll get that!" and grabbed the banana peel, then walked into the office. As I entered, I politely asked if the lady sitting at the desk was the manager in charge; she replied, "Yes... and who the hell are you?"

I replied, "My name is Russell Futcher. I have been sent by the Chairman to find out what the hell is going on here, and now I have a pretty good idea. I will make this quick and easy; you have 15 minutes to pack your bag and leave the premises — you won't be coming back. If you are not out of here by then, I will have security escort you out; it is your choice." Her face turned ashen with disbelief, and her mouth was agog, but realizing she had been caught red-handed, she started to collect the papers off her desk. With that, I turned to go and find the young lady who had been directed to chase the banana peel, who had overheard the conversation. I took her aside and apologized profusely for the behavior she had been subjected to. I asked her if she would be forgiving enough to allow me an opportunity to make things better for her and the employees, and I promised that things would be very different from now on and finished by giving her the rest of the day off.

On speaking to the employees, many of whom I knew, as I had originally set up and staffed this data center, I discovered they too had regularly been subjected to disrespectful and humiliating comments. They were the playthings of the banana lady and some of her staff.

The biggest problem with the Traditional model is that you have managers working within a strict hierarchy with intimidating people in positions of power, who can be coercive, dictatorial, distrusting and treat their staff as subordinates with little value. Employees are growing frustrated at not having input into their work, and they frequently leave when better opportunities arise. Employees are insisting on higher levels of job satisfaction and want their managers to be open and honest, fair and reasonable and to value them and their contributions.

The new Millennial workforce is demanding that their managers act in a collaborative, supportive and motivational manner. They are expressing that they will not accept the old command and control approach, which they view as being more like managing and directing versus leading, and they consider Traditional management to be suffocating, unreasonable and unnecessary. Millennials respond favorably to a newer Transformational leadership style, where free-thinking, empowerment, service and community are put ahead of self-interest. This newer model satisfies their desire to work across teams and their need for feedback and praise. No matter how they are viewed, the simple truth is that Millennials look at work quite differently than their predecessors.

A research study on American employees from Gallup found that 50% resign due to bad management. The study continues to show that having a 'bad' boss creates unhappiness in the office, adding stress and spreading negativity to their home life and families. Finally, workers feel like they're given little guidance as to what's expected of them.

It's time for things to change. The Traditional way of managing has run its course. Increasing competition and rapid changes in technology are fortunately starting to move it into the background. Progressive leaders have known for decades that the Traditional, hierarchical pyramid model is outdated. It does not suit today's fast-moving environment, nor does it suit today's employees. Its rigidity cannot support agility, speed or engagement, and then there is the troubling aspect of vesting of too much, often abusive, power in managers over their employees.

Maren Fox of Berrett Koehler believes that progressive organizations and leaders are motivated by improving the well-being of people and communities in ways that have lasting, intrinsic value. A progressive management style is marked by transparency and sharing information with employees, and that progressive leaders empower everyone and increase collaboration. Progressive leadership offers a clear alternative to the traditional, command-and-control model that has dominated the leadership model conversation for so long. It is a leadership style that values sharing and collaboration.

> In an employee survey, management transparency was the number one factor contributing to employee job satisfaction. In that same survey, teams and collaboration were placed as the top attributes that employees valued about their peers." - by Maren Fox – Berrett Koehler, 2018,

Progressive organizations use the newer Transformational Leadership model.

According to Bernard M. Basa, author and researcher on Transformational Leadership, Transformational leaders tend to be more charismatic, and they are excellent motivators able to get people to do more than they thought possible. He goes on to say, "these leaders inspire followers with challenge and persuasion, providing meaning and understanding; they are intellectually stimulating. The leader is individually considerate, admired, respected and trusted with high standards of ethical and moral conduct. They actively mentor and coach. Creativity is encouraged, with no room for public criticism of individual members' mistakes. They pay special attention to each individual's needs for achievement and growth, and their behavior demonstrates acceptance of individual differences."

Transformational leaders motivate their employees to do more than they thought was possible. They set challenging expectations and typically achieve higher performance outcomes from their employees. They manage people as valuable individuals, identifying and developing their talents. They are supportive, encouraging and motivational. They are role models who are respected and trusted, and they build high-performance teams.

My first experience of a Transformational leadership style was at a progressive insurance and banking group, who engaged me as a member of their IT management team. It was also my introduction to membership of a high-performance team. My new boss, the

Chief Information Officer, was a Transformational-style leader. He was a man with high energy and charisma. On my first day, he welcomed me with a "Hello," then immediately asked his assistant to show me where I could sit. His assistant took me to an office, told me I was now the Applications Development Manager and that all of the 80 employees outside were reporting to me. That was it. A Transformational leader gives you their complete trust, their total support when asked for and empowers you to do whatever you need to do. Accordingly, I had little need to speak to my boss, other than at a weekly management team meeting.

I soon discovered that my peers and fellow management team members were all operating the same way. There was one fundamental difference that I had never encountered before: my peers were concerned that I should do well and continuously offered their unconditional support whenever I should need it. They expected the same in return. This new style of managing and working was a revelation for me, and I thrived.

Over five years, this team produced extraordinary results and excelled at everything it turned its attention to. It created new ways of working, new industry standards and could manage a workload that would simply kill off any other team. The job satisfaction level was off the chart, as was the professional growth and learnings. Massive change was constant and welcomed, innovation was the norm and all during a period of corporate expansion, where a new company was regularly being added to the corporate group. This was a high-performance team created by a Transformational leader.

In 2007, I decided to do something radical. I found a job in Papua New Guinea (PNG) as the Head of Technology for the country's largest IT provider. PNG is a developing country, which means below third-world status. There is a great deal of poverty, violence and hardship. The nationals grow up in a village setting and have a collective consciousness. They are hardworking and intelligent people, even though there are high illiteracy rates due to many people having little-to-no schooling.

Just about everything you can think of at this company needed fixing. I inherited 150 employees, and after arriving, I wondered what the hell I had gotten myself into. Technology aside, everything else was utterly foreign; the language was different, and respecting local customs wasn't just important, it was vital. I learned on my first day that a wrong word or comment could have disastrous consequences, when I innocently made a remark about grass huts and received looks of utter death. I had never before felt so exposed or vulnerable. I worked harder every day at this company than I had ever done before.

The company had a conservative Traditional management model, which was being harshly applied, with employees being treated appallingly and like servants. I even had employees who called me "master." I had my work cut out for me. In the business units that I managed, I used a Transformational management approach for everything I did while building high-performance teams. My business units had to coexist with others that were still being managed in a Traditional style. I learned that the Transformational model could be used in a non-Western environment and under the harshest of business conditions. It could not only coexist with, but it also complemented the older Traditional model. The results and outcomes achieved were genuinely surprising and were enhanced by the employees' village culture of collaboration and shared decision making.

The introduction of formal training alone yielded incredible results, with some employees (trained as computer engineers) receiving awards from the American computer manufacturer, Hewlett Packard.

The Transformational approach, combined with the building of high-performance teams, yielded considerable personal and professional benefits for the employees and the company alike. The key outcomes were that people's lives were fundamentally changed for the better, they had job security, something they had never had before, and their job satisfaction was much higher. Their villages also benefitted. Many of the employees received formal training certifications, something of great value in a society of this kind and something that helped guarantee future employment opportunities. Productivity went up, the balance sheet went from red to black and customer service vastly improved.

All I did was provide training, empowerment, support and motivation. The employees did the rest; all they had needed was a leadership style that would accept them as they were and allow them to use their considerable natural talents. The former Traditional model they had worked under crushed all of their natural abilities and instincts, as well as degraded them daily. It prevented a significant pool of talent from achieving its full potential.

The day I left, after having worked there for five years, many of the employees cried. I never know what to make of that; it had never happened before. I reminded them that they had done the work, not me, and I left knowing that the changes were sustainable. It was one of the best periods of my life, and I miss all of the people dearly.

The use of a Transformational leadership style, combined with the use of high-performance teams, also positively influenced the behaviors of the Traditional managers to be more open, collaborative and far more considerate towards the needs and development of their employees.

The values of the Baby Boomers generation were based on a strong work ethic, respect for authority, loyalty, strong financial management, long-term planning and delayed gratification. Now, we have the rise of the Millennial generation who have grown up with parents from an overworked era and have seen strain/stress grow before their eyes. Having seen this, the Millennials have a desire for work that means something and work which they are heavily contributing to. Therefore, this work needs to create happiness, and if this cannot be fulfilled within the workplace, then the generation will seek satisfaction elsewhere.

> Research conducted by the Institute of Leadership and Management (ILM) discovered that 32% of recent graduates were dissatisfied with their boss' performance and 56% of graduates cited their 'ideal' manager as a coach or mentor figure.

They are a generation who want to be fulfilled within the workplace, while still having time to run with things they are passionate about. This is a new generation that cannot be compared to previous generations, where learning and professional development are essential to them. A flexible work-life balance is a strong, driving desire.

The new generation of Millennials is changing the business world. Information is now the most prized commodity and creative thinking the most sought-after skill, and Millennials have the latter in spades. Millennial workforce expectations do not fit with the Traditional model; this model fails them completely. Unlike the Baby Boomers before them, Millennials are not prepared to be quiet about this, and they are making their feelings known about their attitudes towards work and their expectations about how they want to be treated at work.

Today's management can use this profile to their advantage. They can learn to manage each employee as a unique team member and establish a leadership approach that suits them best. The more approachable a manager can be with employees, the more relaxed the Millennial employee will be, and therefore, they will be more motivated to perform well for their bosses because of their increased respect and regard for them. Millennials are looking for managers who are interested in their professional development and an inclusive organizational culture that rewards individual achievement and promotes on merit rather than tenure.

A consistent and interactive management style works best for this generation, as well as regular, open conversations that involve the worker in their progress. Millennials crave responsibility and involvement within the workplace. Feedback is vital. Millennials need comments about their work, reviews and suggestions for how to do better, especially if they are looking to progress to management. Teamwork is high on the agenda of Millennials, and regular team meetings and collaboration with colleagues are essential. They need openness and transparency from management within an organization.

The fact of the matter is that the new Millennial workforce needs can be completely satisfied by the Transformational leadership model and the use of high-performance teams, both being enormously compatible with their needs and wants as against the old Traditional model.

After my PNG experience, I couldn't stop thinking about why more organizations were not moving to a Transformational leadership model. It occurred to me that there is no established pathway from the old to the new, that is, from the Traditional to the Transformational. A transitional approach and model were needed to bridge the gap and allow for a staged migration. Organizations need time to manage such a significant change, and I determined this is best done organically by the building of high-performance teams within Traditional organizations. What was needed was a formal, transitional management model that combined Transformational leadership with the establishment of high-performance teams, just as I experienced at the insurance and banking group and in PNG.

I developed such a model and called it High-Performance Management and Teams.

This transitional model is based on the Transformational leadership style to progressively create a high-performance organization. Under this model, the concepts of leadership and management are transposable and are not just integral; they are the same. The model works by building high-performance teams as the vehicle for crossing the pathway between the old and the new. It trains all levels of management in high-performance management methods and techniques, bringing about the advent of the high-performance manager, with an emphasis on people leadership skills. The management style is transformational, transparent, and places people first. It creates high levels of mutual trust, mutual accountability, and collaboration. Open communication is a key feature, as is the concept of shared leadership. One of the key benefits of this model is that it does away with any opportunity for management abuse; it quickly identifies and facilitates the calling out of managers who are trying to manage with compulsion and force.

The model recognizes that employees are demanding and deserving of higher levels of job satisfaction and trains managers to be open and honest, fair and reasonable and to value their employees' contributions. It supports employees' demands for recognition of their efforts, their need for a collaborative environment, and allows employees to have a say in how their workplace is managed.

Teams, on the other hand, are driven by the need to be more competitive and by changes in business technology. However, Traditional teams' organizational structures have limitations; they are silo-based and are almost exclusively project-driven, facilitating only existing skillsets. They do not employ modern management behaviors, methods or techniques, and they largely just reinvent as against genuinely innovate.

High-performance teams do not suffer from these restrictions. Team members have complementary skills and can change roles, and leadership is not restricted to an individual. In a high-performance team, the manager acts as the role model who aligns commitment with a common goal and individual performance goals. There are robust methods of resolving conflict, shared norms and values, a strong sense of accountability and high levels of mutual trust. The team shares a collective consciousness and has clearly defined roles and responsibilities, team rules and behaviors. Team members are fully empowered and held accountable.

Finally, the model covers the people change process and provides training on a range of high-performance behaviors, methods and techniques, covering team bonding, time management, personal performance and productivity improvement and most importantly, how to support and motivate.

Team Members can expect significant job satisfaction, more expansive career opportunities, comradery, and being the best in their chosen field. They receive professional development and acquisition of new management skills, over time becoming increasingly better at whatever is being done and developing the ability to overachieve in comparison to others.

The benefits to the organization are becoming an employer of choice, staff loyalty, increased competitiveness, profits, ability to expand rapidly, market growth and having teams focused on business needs. Add to these: reduced costs, improved performance, efficiency and productivity, improved services and product quality, as well as better service delivery and technical capability.

Today, progressive organizations are leading the way in respect of how they view people management; it is these organizations that are making the move to Transformational management and the use of high-performance teams. Progress, however, is painfully slow. Perhaps the publishing of this chapter might help move things along with the use of the pathway I have created. I will leave you with this question to ponder: Do you want to work (or have your children work) in a Traditionally managed organization, where personal and professional opportunity is limited or delayed? Or, would you rather work in a progressive organization that values people as their greatest asset, and employs transformational and high-performance management methods?

"Leadership is about making others better as a result of your presence and making sure that impact lasts in your absence."

~ Sheryl Sandberg

CHAPTER ELEVEN

Cultivating the Awakened Leader Within

By Ciara Mc Ardle

S omething very interesting happened in the midst of editing this chapter, which significantly changed what I will share with you now. I had written and previously submitted a completely different first draft at the end of November 2020. I intended to refine this draft to better reflect the immensity of what I perceive the *New Paradigm of Leadership* to be, as I felt that I had only shared the tip of the iceberg on this topic.

When it was time to dive into the editing process, I experienced my first big bout of writer's block and found it hard to even open my laptop. I stepped away from the process for a day and woke up the following morning with renewed inspiration and clarity, ready to dive in.

I was then shocked to discover that my laptop was no longer operable! It was doing all sorts of crazy things. First, it was hard to switch on. I persevered and was elated to hear the familiar sound of the desktop opening chime through. However, then the dimming button would, of its own accord, go to full dimming so that the screen was in darkness. I managed to get the screen lit up again, and when I brought my draft onto the screen, the words started wandering around by themselves. It finally settled, and I started the editing process. However, the delete button then would not work! Bewildered, again, I had to step back.

With so many obstacles occurring, I knew not to push it. I took some deep breaths and decided to reach out to a friend to reflect on these strange occurrences. She kept repeating one piece of advice, which I totally did not want to hear. Her advice was to put my original draft aside, meditate to center and align myself and allow the writing to flow through onto a fresh, clear, blank screen! I had no intention of starting all over again. Regardless, she gave me her laptop so I could continue with the process.

That evening, I did a strong healing meditation to clear anything within me or within my energy field that may have been interfering with my writing. I then curled up to sleep that night, totally unsuspecting of what was to come…

In the middle of the night, I am jolted out of my sleep. My body temperature is really hot. It feels like I am burning up… I am perceiving the words:

"Radical times call for radical measures … No time to play small… Radical times call for radical measures. Allow 'Her' to speak through you. Her voice needs to be heard. Don't hold back. Don't give in to fear. Her wisdom needs to be heard. It is time!"

I hesitate at first. It is 2:36 am on Friday, 8th January 2021. My eyes are still blurry from having been fast asleep. Somehow, before I allowed my mind to take over, the urgency of the message got me to grab my friend's laptop. I take a few moments to center myself. With the laptop open, I try to tune into my inner world and see what I could perceive.

In my meditation, I see a circle around me of who I recognize to be several Divine Feminine Ascended Masters. They look toward the center at the One Sophia. She wants to speak through me, and I wait to see what she wants to say. I falter. Is this real? Am I really going to be able to allow Her to speak through me? I bow my head and tune in.

I started typing, and the words flowed through me effortlessly for two hours nonstop! The floodgates had opened. I did my best to put my ego and questioning mind aside to be open to what wanted to be communicated so urgently.

This is not a practice that I had ever experienced before. However, recently I had begun to develop an *inner ear* for messages to be received. I would start with the intention to tune into any inner guidance that wanted to be communicated, quiet my mind and then start to write. As I wrote, the words would just flow and a message would form in my journal. This time it was very different. I had not initiated the session. I was literally woken up in the middle of the night and very strongly told to start typing!

Essentially, it was what you might call a download, a channeling, a transmission or some might like to refer to it as tapping into the subconscious mind. In this case, however, this message did seem to come from a being outside myself, who was referred to as the One Sophia. She clearly wanted to communicate on the topic of *New Paradigm Leadership*, yet she spoke about it from a much broader and higher perspective-than I would have written about.

Over the course of those two hours, many messages poured through. She shifted the perspective of new paradigm leadership into the wider context of humanity being in the midst of massive paradigm shifts across all facets of life on earth.

She highlighted, however, that we are very much still in the transitional stages of moving from one paradigm to another. She acknowledges the extremely difficult times and hardships that people are facing because of the virus and lockdowns, but alongside this, she brings a strong message of hope. She gets quite prophetic and foretells that life on earth will look very different, in a really good way, after a period of time.

She stresses the point that a lot of work is needed in order to fully shift into and align with the new paradigms. She refers to a particular group of people/leaders that many will look to for support and guidance in these transitional times.

All of this information was a lot to take in, but it felt right. It was quite humbling and felt like a gift. I deliberated for a short while on what to do with it. Yet, there is nothing that I disagree with or would choose to omit. It felt like a huge relief, like something had been given birth through me. Although there is vulnerability in sharing material like this, after some reflection, I concluded, who am I not to share it? It seemed clear that the messages that came through were totally relevant to this book.

So, I have shared the material below in its original form; aside from adding in some subheadings to make for easier reading and some very minor editing. Much of the channeling speaks for itself, and there are multiple messages and layers in there. In the subsequent section, I will be sharing from my own perspective and life experience. I'll be tying in my views on *new paradigm leadership* with respect to some of the key points in the channeling, with the aim of giving more context, practical examples and suggestions to further integrate this material.

I will leave it up to you, the reader, to receive all of this as an offering. Take what resonates, and if something does not resonate or make sense to you, please leave it aside. You may feel drawn to come back to it at a later date and then see it in a fresh, new light.

[Incidentally, after taking my laptop to a repair shop, I had been told that I would need to wipe the hard drive and replace the keyboard. After handing in the new draft and receiving back the fresh, new edited version, I decided to give my laptop another try. Although not perfect, I could completely do the editing on it, and the further I refined the writing, the more my computer came fully back online!]

Sophia Speaks:

"I know this is new for you, dear one, but please keep writing. Don't look up to edit. Let it flow.

We are indeed at a time of a great shift. Old paradigms are fast falling away. This has all been preordained. So much work has been done on multiple dimensions for this time. Indeed, there is a battle being played out, but the forces of light are unstoppable. Some turbulence has been experienced and will continue to be experienced in the following months as the darkness prevailing on the earth for centuries fights its final battles. It cannot win any longer. What plays out on the higher dimensions needs time to filter down onto your earth plane.

People amongst you - the light-workers, star-seeds, planetary workers - have exceeded our expectations and have helped the planet activate the highest timelines culminating in the New Earth's birthing. There is much to celebrate."

A Great Shift in Consciousness

"We know it does not look like that at present from where you stand. Indeed, there is much suffering happening on your planet as the virus and subsequent lockdowns wreak havoc across the earth. Yet much has been done in the unseen realms that will soon become apparent to all. Indeed, you are at a time where radical change is needed. As many of you know, and what many are soon to become aware of, is that we are in times of a great shift in consciousness. The old ways are no longer sustainable. It is time that people open up to access higher dimensions of their Being, where new ways of operating, perceiving and living can become apparent.

For too long, systems of oppression, repression and distortion have reigned on your planet. No longer can this paradigm sustain itself. Your planet was on a path of self-destruction and it needed to be stopped. Something radical had to happen to wake people out of their slumber and start recognizing who they are and what the new potentials are. Soon more will realize that we are at the dawn of a great awakening. Balance and the light are returning to your planet. Many unpleasant truths need to be witnessed to see how far out of balance things have become.

For too long, the feminine voice and wisdom have been distorted and written out of history. The distorted masculine of domination, power-over, manipulation and control has gone on for so long. There has been much suffering. It will be hard for many to comprehend the levels of darkness and deception that were at play. Know that in all of the darkness coming to the surface, much

174

is being healed, transformed and brought back to the light so that these atrocities can never play out again.

Astrologically, with the planetary alignments, many of you who are awake are seeing and recognizing this great shift. The energies, frequencies and planetary alignments you are now in no longer support the old energies. Fear of lack, greed, control and manipulation can no longer play out in these new energies. Anything out of alignment with the higher good of the planet will soon be unsustainable. Any system that is not acting for the highest good of all concerned will not survive."

A New Earth

"Naturally, those who are in alignment with these new energies will begin to thrive. There is so much waiting to come in to serve a collective vision of actually creating heaven on earth. Many innovations that were suppressed in the old paradigm will now be able to come forward. Free energy, new financial systems where there is more than enough for all and sustainable ways of living symbiotically with the environment will become the new norm.

People will come from a space of love and connection. Trust will replace fear. Abundance will replace scarcity. You will naturally thrive as opposed to competing to merely survive. People will establish heart-centered communities and allow everyone to develop their natural gifts and wisdom. Innovations in health and wellness will come. Quantum medicine and the understanding of humans as energy beings will create health for all."

Sovereign Leaders

"No longer will duality tear your societies and planet apart. Government parties of the left-wing and right-wing, democratic and republic, liberal versus conservative, were in endless battles that took energy away from what truly mattered, serving the highest good of all the people. Each person will be a sovereign leader, empowered in their own unique design and serving the collective. People will naturally have a sense of responsibility towards themselves, their families, communities, countries and the planet. They will not need dominating laws to control their behaviors. Naturally, they will collectively come up with solutions to the various challenges that lie ahead."

Masculine/Feminine Balance

"In essence, there will be a healthy balance of the masculine and the feminine ways of operating. A balance will come in between 'doing' and 'being.' For too long, your people have been caught up in ways of 'doing' running around without questioning or connecting deeper within themselves. This has led to burnout, disconnection and people living lives without a deeper sense of purpose or meaning. This will all change."

New Leadership Paradigm

"Indeed, leadership will look so different. Replacing the hierarchical, predominantly masculine ways of organizing systems will be a more feminine, collective way of collaborating, listening, discussing and general tuning into the best ways to serve the collective good. Every person's contribution will be valued. People will be more in tune with their inner wisdom, and clarity

and solutions will be found easily as people surrender to this higher wisdom. No longer will so much be segregated, spirit and matter, mind and heart, left and right brain.

Quantum ways of perceiving and operating will be the new norm. With this wider view, solutions become apparent and new ways of running your societies will naturally form, in sync with nature, communities and spirit. Everything will feed the soul. People will recognize the sacredness in everything and naturally live in a state of peace, joy and equanimity. People will naturally blossom and develop their gifts. They will become natural leaders in their areas of expertise. There will be a synergy among people where everyone brings out the best in the group or shared collective."

Inner Work in the Transition

"In these transitional times, much is needing to be transmuted as you transition out of centuries of pain, suffering, wars, famines, oppression and domination. Those who have been on the path of self-healing are more ready. Many have cleared centuries of abuse, trauma and ancestral pain. They have awakened to being more than they ever thought or dreamt possible before.

Much work is needed in this transition, and you have the tools.

Those who have not been looking within, accessing their inner wisdom and doing the healing work, will need assistance and many are ready to assist, support and empower. They, too, will soon see that there is much to be excited about. The new energies will help with this, as they feel the energies of love, hope and peace surge through them; once the initial shock waves of the revelations and the great awakening pass through.

There is no need to be afraid, and much to celebrate."

Cultivating the Leader Within

"Indeed, a new caliber of leader is emerging. People who are not buying into duality or competing ways of being, who recognize and bring out the wisdom within every human being. Children can be our teachers. They are the teachers of the future. Those being born in recent times are very different. They are born into a different energy and have been able to come in with much higher levels of consciousness. You would bode well to listen to them, learn from them. They will bring much innovation. They are being born into a world where the systems are broken, and they will naturally birth the new ways.

Cultivating the leader within everyone is the new paradigm.

No longer can a few control the strings and have everyone at their bidding. Collective sharing of power and responsibility will naturally arise. You will awaken out of the belief of scarcity and welcome abundance for all. You will treat your planet with the utmost respect and love that she deserves. People will once again see the sacredness in everything, and she will be allowed to return to balance as you symbiotically learn to live with her. She will teach you as you learn to listen to her wisdom pouring through each vibrant living being."

Dreaming the New Earth into Being

"In this environment, creativity will be the norm and so much will be birthed. You will lift each other up and be excited to create more versions of heaven on earth. What you can dream up now is only a fraction of what will come to pass. Allow this possibility to enter into your consciousness. Flirt with it, breathe with it, see how it plays with you and what it wants to birth through you.

It may take time to adjust to even these possibilities, but these are the new ways. The sooner you can step into your leadership in this, the sooner the cocreations can begin. There is much waiting for you beloveds. You have suffered so much. There has been too much suffering.

We need you all to step into your leadership and begin dreaming this new world into being.

Acknowledge and move through any sense of skepticism or disbelief, and dare to dream, dare to envision what this new earth can look like. We are here now, beloveds. The birthing has begun, yet there is much work to be done.

Stay strong, stay focused. Focus on the limitless possibilities that are waiting for you.

Open more to the Divine. Listen within. It is all inside you. The potential is there.

Will you listen to the call? Will you tap into the leader within?"

- The session lasted for two hours, where I typed nonstop. Afterwards, I closed the laptop and fell back asleep.

In the next section, I will share some of my own journey and insights that will complement, give context to and expand on some of the key points made above.

The recommendations that She gives for the transitional times are very much in line with the work that I facilitate for my clients and what my life journey has been all about!

I will also share some practical suggestions about how we can navigate this great shift into the new paradigm ways of being and leadership.

Cultivating the Awakened Leader Within

- We are so much more than we think we are.

Mystics, Shamans and Enlightened Masters have been speaking about this throughout history, pointing us to something greater within and beyond us. Yogis often spent decades in caves, mastering the art of inner wisdom, greater perception and enlightenment. Yet, for many in the current day, fast-paced modern life, that possibility seems unreal, fanciful or unattainable.

However, I got a glimpse of something profound while on a ten-day silent meditation retreat in a Thai Buddhist Monastery in 1997. Although it was only a taste, I experienced a deeper aspect of my *being* that I had not accessed before. Spontaneous healing and insights around difficult issues in my life arose naturally. My whole perception of reality drastically shifted from then on.

I had many questions. Why wasn't this spoken about back home or taught about in schools? It seemed to me that this type of experience was essential to the very fabric of life. If I could access a taste of this in only ten days, I wondered what was possible if I could tap into this more and integrate it into a way of life back home. Essentially, this experience fueled my life's journey ever since and is a key element of the work I now facilitate for others.

The Buddha spoke about us all having an enlightened nature inside us that is naturally wise, compassionate and kind. The Buddha's teaching would say that our busy minds, emotions and conditioning hide this innate intelligent nature. Similarly, other traditions would say that we are spiritual beings or souls in the human body. Many different teachings point to something wise and profound within us.

Doing the Inner Work

To further integrate this experience and understand more about human nature, I dove into the study of psychology, psychotherapy, healing, quantum science and spirituality on my return home to Ireland. I began to realize that many of us carry unprocessed emotions and trauma in our bodies. Spiritual author, Eckhart Tolle, refers to the unprocessed emotional pain, that we carry around with us, as the *pain-body*. This pain-body is like dirty glasses that we look at the world through, making us feel numb and disconnected, or distorting how we view and react to situations, which can cause some drama and unnecessary chaos in our lives.

After many years on this path, both with myself and in facilitating others, I found that the more we do the inner work (shadow work, trauma healing, self-reflection, etc.) to heal the layers in our pain-body, the more aspects of ourselves we reclaim and the more integrated, whole and empowered we feel. A wise and compassionate sense of inner direction and self-leadership often arises as a result. The benefits of becoming more self-aware and doing our inner work are not only for us but for all those around us: our children, our relationships and our societies.

Particularly, if someone in a leadership role has not spent any time in self-reflection and developed any awareness of their inner world, they can cause a lot of stress and trauma to those around them, often unconsciously. We all know examples of bosses who come into the workplace full of irritation, frustration or anxiety, and then project that out onto the team of people they work with. That is neither a pleasant nor productive environment to be in, regardless of what type of leader they are or what leadership style they are practicing.

The Hero's Journey

Many are propelled on soul-searching inner journeys only in times of crisis. Depending on the severity of the crisis, we may first descend into what is referred to as a "dark night of the soul." During these challenging times, you could say that we have primarily two options available to us. The first is to wallow in a lot of negativity, reactivity and blame, arising from our resistance to the suffering that we are faced with. The second is to open up and surrender to *what is*. When we surrender to and fully face the situation, what often happens is that we drop deep within ourselves and find the resources to start the healing and rebuilding processes. What usually follows is a sense of strength when we have passed through the eye of the storm and made it out the other side, feeling more resilient than ever before.

Joseph Campbell recognized this journey as an archetypal pattern that many of us go through, which he aptly named *The Hero's Journey*. If we think about our favorite novels and movies, we can often see this archetypal journey underlying the main plot.

"The Hero's Journey was the story of the man or woman who, through great suffering, reached an experience of the eternal source and returned with gifts powerful enough to set their society free."
~ Wikipedia (Joseph Campbell)

Eckhart Tolle, and many other awakened leaders in the spiritual growth movement, would describe their awakening journeys in a similar way. Eckhart talks about sleeping on a park bench, having been depressed and suicidal. He got to a point where he dropped all resistance to his experience and opened to the full extent that he was suffering. He suddenly had a profound awakening and shift in his reality, where he experienced and understood life from a completely different perspective. His depression lifted as he felt states of inner joy, peace and wisdom. Since then, this shift in consciousness has remained, and he has become one of the most prominent spiritual leaders of modern times.

Another woman who I have personally met had a profound awakening in a Japanese prison. She suffered greatly, physically from horrendous nerve pain, and psychologically from being in a foreign jail for an unknown length of time with hostile inmates. She had gotten herself into solitary confinement purposely to have her own space. She reached a point where she could no longer resist feeling the pain. She dropped in and felt all the layers of the pain. As she dropped deeper into the layers, she reached a point where it opened into a powerful light… and she was free. From then on, it didn't matter if she was in prison or not. She felt a deep peace and freedom inside her that could not be affected by any outer circumstances.

"There is a point where only surrender to what is, is the point when you can become free of suffering."
~ Eckhart Tolle in "Become Awake Now!" video conversations with Russell Brand.

Facilitating a Gentler Way

Thankfully, we do not all need to go to such extremes to have healing and awakening experiences. I learned that if we do the work to connect to our inner world and listen to the inner nudges, intuition and impulses, we can awaken to something powerful within us with more ease and grace!

In the work that I facilitate for others, I am very excited to have found tools and practices to guide people on their healing journeys, assisting them to access their inner wisdom and essence. By creating a healing space using certain key components, often it seems that just by a simple change in perspective or a gentle nudge in the right direction, something profound opens up. What follows never ceases to amaze me. As I guide them, they get into a flow of speaking from the space of their inner wisdom. Subsequently, they often effortlessly come up with all the answers, solutions and insights that they originally had difficulty with!

Unprecedented Times

We are in such a turbulent time right now. 2020 will be forever etched in our memories as the unprecedented year that changed everything. The whole of humanity has been affected by it. We are still "in it." We are all having our own unique experiences, and there are many differing and conflicting opinions about what is going on and how it should be handled. Regardless of what we believe or feel about it, reality as we knew it has been shaken to its core. The world is currently in a global crisis, and there is much uncertainty. Many people are suffering from stress and trauma, confused and in fear of what lies ahead. The pressure cooker is being turned up on many aspects of life.

Essentially, we are on a collective Hero's Journey. It is a time when we need to be drawing on all our resources, individually and collectively. Now, more than ever, we need strong, emotionally balanced, resilient and visionary leaders in our world, in all levels and facets of our society. We need to draw on all the resources, insights and tools that we can access.

I don't believe that it is merely a coincidence that this book, sharing many insights on new paradigm leadership, has come into being at this time and that you are reading it, right now.

Great Awakening

What then of the messages that came through with such urgency in the middle of the night? The channeling points to something that is happening right now, parallel to all the suffering that we see in our world today.

In their essence, the messages bring hope. They seem to imply that even though we are currently experiencing a lot of global hardship, that something new and beautiful is emerging at the same time. She talks about us now being in a time of a Great Awakening where a Global Shift in Consciousness is occurring.

Many who have been on personal and spiritual growth journeys over the last few decades recognize these shifts that are happening. Wise, ancient traditions have spoken about this time for eons. They knew the impact that powerful astrological alignments would have on the earth. They could see through the mapping of the "procession of the equinoxes" that a 26,000-year cycle would be coming to completion. They foresaw that these alignments would affect massive shifts in paradigms across all facets of life on earth. They also predicted that many organizational structures on the planet would need to be restructured, and that many old ways of doing things would no longer be aligned to the new energies and consciousness.

These astrological alignments that they speak of mean that higher frequencies of light and energy are streaming onto the earth. This has a direct impact on our physical, mental, emotional, soul and energetic levels. If we think of everything in terms of frequency and energy, when the light shines on lower frequencies of energy (denser energies, such as heavier emotions of pain, fear, guilt, shame, control and trauma), it will bring them up to the surface to be seen, healed and released. This is just like when we pour water into a glass containing oil, the water will push the oil (which is denser) to the surface, where it will eventually spill out of the glass.

This is why Sophia stressed the importance of everyone doing their inner work, to heal and clear their pain bodies in order to better adapt to the new energies and to be able to align with deeper aspects of their being.

To some, it will seem that things are getting worse in terms of how they feel. However, what may have taken years in therapy in the older energies will now be able to be processed much faster. The energies will also be illuminating our inner essence, the divine spark within, making that more accessible. I am witnessing this a lot in the sessions that I facilitate. The shifts and healing can happen quite effortlessly. The key is to be open to doing the healing work; to both clear what no longer serves us and tap into more aspects of our being that we may not have accessed before.

Thankfully, there are so many tools, modalities and practices that can be availed of. Various spiritual practices like meditation, mindfulness and yoga can bring us into a place of more awareness, balance and clarity, to allow inner wisdom and intuition to arise. Learning how to deregulate a stressed, nervous system and create resilience will no doubt save lives. Many trauma-informed practices are now available, as well as a proliferation of support groups, types of psychotherapy, counseling, healing and embodiment practices.

It is highly likely that we will see a rise in people developing extrasensory gifts, where they would be able to access that which is beyond the five senses, i.e., clairvoyance (seeing), clairaudience (hearing), clairsentience (feeling), precognition, etc. For example, I would never have thought that I would be up in the middle of the night downloading information and messages through clairaudience that I would then consider sharing with others!

The potentials are enormous. It means that the awakening process is no longer only accessible to a select few yogis who hide away and meditate in caves for years. Embodying our Higher Self can become the new norm. What would most likely follow from that, as Sophia points to, would be enlightened societies. There would be less place or tolerance for wars, greed, control and manipulation. People would instead foster communities from compassion, empowerment, peace, integrity, joy and harmony.

Currently, there are many people who have been walking the path of healing, evolution and awakening for years, while others are awakening every day. They are the ones who are now being called to step up and take conscious leadership roles in all facets of society. They are being asked to assist, support and empower others to integrate these new energies and shifts in consciousness so that we can all cocreate the new paradigms.

We are in such powerful times. I hope and trust that the information here is helpful to you on your personal journey.

I recommend that you consider the suggestions given in the transmission, to tap into the deeper wisdom and love within you and dare to dream up a world that you would love to live in!

"We need you all to step into your leadership and begin dreaming this new world into being."

"Stay strong, stay focused. Focus on the limitless possibilities that are waiting for you.

Open more to the Divine. Listen within. It is all inside you. The potential is there.

Will you listen to the call? Will you tap into the leader within?"

"Before you are a leader, success is all about growing yourself. When you become a leader, success is all about growing others."

~ Jack Welch

Author Biographies

Debi Beebe

CHAPTER ONE

Debi Beebe built an extremely successful career in the fitness and nutrition industry for 30 years by being a private trainer to celebrity clientele. She was a fitness model, is a black belt in Tae Kwon Do and a certified Tae Bo instructor.

After semi-retiring, she discovered a Health and Wellness network marketing company aligned with her values. She became fired up and went to work, helping as many people as she could to increase their health and their wealth globally. She quickly reached millionaire status within the company. Debi made her way to become one of the most powerful women in network marketing, speaking on international stages and running trainings about business and mindset.

Over the years, she realized that empowering people is one of her most essential purposes, starting with our mindset. Debi Beebe is the creator of Manage Your Mindset Monday, a biweekly platform that mentors upcoming leaders and anyone who wants to achieve more in their life. She truly strives to support others to be difference-makers.

Being a Difference Maker in all areas, and giving back is one of the most significant ways to show love on a bigger scale. Debi, her husband Jeff and their adult children and granddaughter give their time and resources to the beloved company's IsaFoundation and The Ronald McDonald House. This is true fulfillment.

"Health is our Wealth, and Wealth is our Health, and the two cannot be divided."

Contact information: debibeebe.me or debibeebe@gmail.com .

Izaak Coetzee

CHAPTER TWO

Strategist, Leadership and Transformation Coach

Izaak Coetzee is a seasoned professional with over 20 years of Senior Management and Executive experience. His expertise overarches positions in compliance, governance, regulatory, strategy and business transformation in government and publicly listed companies. He holds an MBA degree and is the Head of Strategy for one of Africa's biggest telcos.

Izaak is a certified Neuro Leadership coach and an internationally certified NLP Practitioner. He also specializes as an Enneagram Practitioner.

Complimenting his corporate career, Izaak has been coaching and mentoring for more than ten years with a strong focus on leadership development. He has deep experience in mediation, negotiations and conflict management within the business environment.

His unique skill set and business experience allow him to integrate this with a neuro leadership approach to unleash his clients' potential. His experience lies in the areas of executive coaching, leadership development, as well as personal transformation.

He harnesses the ability to think outside of the box and inspires creative, innovative and real-world solutions that support his clients. Practical support is provided in integrating aspects of business and self - through greater levels of self-awareness and the associated shifts in thinking, relationships and action.

With a natural ability to connect and inspire others, Izaak easily relates to people from all walks of life and all levels of experience. He is a confident and vibrant leader who believes that everyone has untapped potential, lying in wait to be uncovered.

Kim Wen

CHAPTER THREE

K im Wen is a recognized and respected authority in the corporate training industry.

With deep expertise in sales, systems design thinking and team development, she knows how to develop a range of business skills to achieve a higher level of personal/team understanding, cohesiveness, and productivity.

As a mentor, advisor and professional business coach, Kim has an up-close and personal perspective of the challenges leaders face in this rapidly changing world. Her employment with large corporations in Australia, Asia and America, allows her to possess a strong perspective of the concerns leaders are now wrestling with.

Author of the phenomenally successful Black Belt Entrepreneur and Property Secrets books. Kim is able to draw out insight, empower, motivate and inspire a collaborative and inclusive approach to group decision making and problem-solving in diverse settings. Kim has established and runs successful SME's, locally.

Her group integrated program focusing on personal and team behavioral change has been recognized with an SME business award.

Her qualifications include branding study at Columbia University, Degrees in Finance, Information Technology and International Trade, Accreditation as a Blair Singer (Rich Dad Poor Dad Advisor) Certified Senior Coach and recognition as an MDA expert.

Outside of work, Kim is a wife, a mother, distance runner, hiker and an active member of her community.

Stefan Almér

CHAPTER FOUR

Stefan Almér is the boy who grew up on a farm, with no aspiration to become a leader but curiosity from a voice inside to discover more of his own potential. Forty years later, through several life experiences and leadership roles, he is now working as a leadership and business development coach/advisor from his company, STAYFUN.

His expertise lies in the depth of understanding how to support people and organizations unfolding the true hidden essence of heart-centered leadership and being as a person, and bringing these two together to reveal the hidden potential of the self and the organization.

Stefan's experience is diverse, from business innovation and leadership to energy work, personal development and frequency guidance. He has had top-level manager roles in both the private and official sectors within Digitalization, Research and Development, Sustainability and Human Resources.
You can read more about Stefan at www.stayfundevelopment.se

John Spender

CHAPTER FIVE

John Spender is a 23-time international best-selling co-author, who didn't learn how to read and write at a basic level until he was ten years old. He has since traveled the world, started many businesses, leading him to create the best-selling book series, *A Journey of Riches*. He is an award-winning international speaker and movie maker.

John worked as an international NLP trainer and has coached thousands of people from various backgrounds through all sorts of challenges. From the borderline homeless to very wealthy individuals, he has helped many people to get in touch with their truth to create a life on their terms.

John's search for answers to live a fulfilling life has taken him to work with Native American Indians in the Hills of San Diego, the forests of Madagascar, swimming with humpback whales in Tonga, exploring the Okavango Delta of Botswana and the Great Wall of China. He's traveled from Chile to Slovakia, Hungary to the Solomon Islands, the mountains of Italy and the streets of Mexico.

Everywhere his journey has taken him, John has discovered a hunger among people to find a new way to live, with a yearning for freedom of expression. His belief that everyone has a book in them was born.

He is now a writing coach, having worked with more than 200 authors from 40 different countries for the *A Journey of Riches* series http://ajourneyofriches.com/, and his publishing house, Motion Media International has published 28 non-fiction titles to date.

John also co-wrote and produced the movie documentary *Adversity*, starring Jack Canfield, Rev. Micheal Bernard Beckwith, Dr. John Demartini and many more, coming soon in 2020. Moreover, you can bet there will be a best-selling book to follow!

Elizabeth Jennifer Chua

CHAPTER SIX

E lizabeth Chua is an educator, a wife and a student of life. She has had the privilege of working and mentoring youths for the past seven years and she is not ready to stop! She has been practicing public speaking for five years, allowing her to not only brush up her skills but also dive deep into an extensive range of topics. Topics that fire up Elizabeth are ones on self-improvement and leadership.

Elizabeth absolutely enjoys reading and learning, creating music and spending time with her loved ones. Her goals for life is to live to the fullest, create and serve with love. One of her favorite quotes that she lives by is, "Let us love, since that is what our hearts were made for" – Saint Therese of Lisieux.

Elizabeth has recently started Labourers of Love, a place where she and her husband share a glimpse of their life along with tips and tricks on how to live your life to the fullest while being a joy to others along the way. You can connect with her on Instagram

@labourers_of_love and head over to www.labourersoflove.sg for awesome resources and entertaining content!

Michelle Gardiner

CHAPTER SEVEN

Michelle is the founder of The Aspire Series and vice president of Restoring Hope, a small Australian-based nonprofit organization. Michelle is a social worker and coach, and has spent over fourteen years working in the child protection sector, supporting children, young people and families through some of their most vulnerable and confronting life experiences. Through hearing and playing a part in many people's life stories, Michelle became most passionate about raising the aspirations of young women and women, which led her to begin The Aspire Series.

Michelle firmly believes that with genuine opportunity, meaningful support and spaces where we can learn to truly love, value and believe in ourselves, that this is where magic is created and where we can become so much bolder than we ever imagined. Michelle also believes that great aspirations must be matched with a great capacity to nurture ourselves, to create the sweet spot where leaders blossom. This is where we can truly influence social change and contribute to our local communities' shifting dynamic and our global society.

Michelle holds a Bachelors of Social and Community Welfare and a Graduate Certificate in Mental Health Science (Child Psychoanalytic Psychotherapy). She is a yoga teacher (500 hours - Moksha Yoga Academy) and she has a background in life coaching, individual and collective narrative work, leadership and empowerment program facilitation and trauma-informed practice.

Lillian Tahuri

CHAPTER EIGHT

Lillian Tahuri lives in Auckland, New Zealand and is from the tribes of Ngati Kahungunu and Ngai Tuhoe. Lillian Tahuri has a background in central and local government, working across strategy, policy, planning, compliance and legislation implementation. She is also a personal development, transformational and leadership coach. Lillian works with individuals and groups to create better leaders on trauma, phobias, high performance and positive mindset tools to improve their clients' lives.

She is passionate about the environment, human rights, gender equality, diversity and inclusion. She has served as a board member on the UN Women Aotearoa New Zealand National Committee and represented the Women's Empowerment Principles Committee (WEPs) board.

Lillian is from New Zealand and has successfully represented her tribe to settle historical claims against their government. She holds a Bachelor of Arts (Humanities) in Philosophy from Massey University in New Zealand, is a Neuro-Linguistic Programming

(NLP) Master Coach, Master Hypnotist and is trained in neuroscience-based personal development.

Mariese B. Vacalares

CHAPTER NINE

Mariese B. Vacalares was born in the City of Golden Friendship, called Cagayan de Oro City, in the Land of Promise – Mindanao, a booming island in southern Philippines.

Inspired by a Fortune Magazine article, she ventured into real estate brokerage and investments, real property leasing and development. She operates a beach resort called Mar Villa Beach, developing facilities for a wellness and wholeness center.

Her healing journey is elaborated in her upcoming book *The Medical Dropout*, where she also became a serial entrepreneur after dropping out of medical school with several MLM businesses, merchandising, trainings and events production and management., workforce, tourism, food and beverage, marketing several products and services carried in her Octagold one-stop business center.

Her wellness advocacies led her to a recent career as a yoga teacher, theta healer, working on her certifications as a life, wellness and transformational coach. Her continuing studies in energy medicine, homeopathy, naturopathy, Ayurveda, quantum, pranic and reiki healing, yoga, NLP, meridian therapy and other alternative or complementary medicine inspires her more into wellness and wholeness.

She's developing Kai'yah as an integrated lifestyle movement and Kaya as a development center in conjunction with her advocacies, a foundation for the helpless and hopeless, and social entrepreneurship to help alleviate poverty in the country.

Contact :
www.facebook.com/mariese.vacalares
octagoldphils@gmail.com ,
Phone +63 9176268095 , Viber, Whatsapp

Russell Futcher

CHAPTER TEN

Russell lives in Melbourne, Australia with his red colored spoodle, Cassie. He owns and operates several businesses based on his many years as a management consultant, specializing in IT where he gained an enviable reputation as a trouble-shooter and someone who gets things done. A very frank and direct guy, he has a talent for discovering and developing hidden talent in people which is what drives him the most.

He has an extensive business background in insurance, banking, health, transport, retail, superannuation and technology sectors and is qualified in Business and Executive Coaching, Management Development and Training and Education. He is the developer of the "IT Best Practice Standards" and the "High-Performance Management and Teams" Management model, and the author of five books and an online management training course.

Russell is also an experienced electronic and print media presenter ,who spends his spare time as a practicing health nut and also researching behavioral dynamics. His favorite subject, he says, is people. "I just like everyone."

Ciara Mc Ardle

CHAPTER ELEVEN

C iara facilitates deeply transformative processes that support and empower people on their healing, embodiment and awakening journeys.

She is a systemic family constellations facilitator, certified TRE® (Trauma Release Exercises) provider, inner dance facilitator, core & cellular healing practitioner and sacred space holder.

Since a profound awakening at a ten-day meditation (Vipassana) retreat in Thailand in 1997, she has passionately been exploring and training in the most effective ways of personal and spiritual transformation across the globe. Ciara has immersed herself in the fields of wellbeing and personal development, ancient healing traditions, alongside cutting-edge science and spiritual wisdom.

She has academic trainings in Science (BSc), Applied Psychology (HDip), Buddhist based Psychotherapy, and Transpersonal / Holistic Counseling (Dip). Since 2000, she has worked in the fields of mental health, addiction, trauma recovery, learning disability (Autism & Aspergers), wellness, personal & spiritual development and co-hosted several retreats across the globe.

She provides a 'Holistic Integrative Healing Approach' drawing on the most effective transformational tools and processes that she has found. She is passionate about working with people on all levels of 'Being', i.e. physical, mental, emotional, energetic, soul and spiritual levels. She also brings in a wider perspective, through systemic constellations, working in the ancestral field and in the quantum field of sacred space.

Although a diverse range of tools and skills, she weaves them together simply to suit the needs of the individual or group that she is working with. You can read more about her offerings here ... https://embodyingessence.weebly.com

"A leader takes people where they want to go. A great leader takes people where they don't necessarily want to go, but ought to be."

~ Rosalynn Carter

Afterword

I hope you enjoyed the collection of heartfelt stories, wisdom and vulnerability shared. Storytelling is the oldest form of communication, and I hope you feel inspired to take a step toward living a fulfilling life. Feel free to contact any of the authors in this book, or the other books in this series.

The proceeds of this book will go to feeding many of the rural Balinese families that are struggling through the current pandemic.

Other books in the series are...

The Attitude of Gratitude : *A Journey of Riches,* Book Twenty Three
https://www.amazon.com/dp/1925919269

Facing your Fears : *A Journey of Riches,* Book Twenty Two
https://www.amazon.com/dp/1925919218

Returning to Love : *A Journey of Riches,* Book Twenty One
https://www.amazon.com/dp/B08C54M2RB

Develop Inner Strength : *A Journey of Riches,* Book Twenty
https://www.amazon.com/dp/1925919153

Building your Dreams : A Journey of Riches, Book Nineteen
https://www.amazon.com/dp/B081KZCN5R

Liberate your Struggles : A Journey of Riches, Book Eighteen
https://www.amazon.com/dp/1925919099

In Search of Happiness : A Journey of Riches, Book Seventeen
https://www.amazon.com/dp/B07R8HMP3K

Tapping into Courage : A Journey of Riches, Book Sixteen
https://www.amazon.com/dp/B07NDCY1KY

The Power Healing : A Journey of Riches, Book Fifteen
https://www.amazon.com/dp/B07LGRJQ2S

The Way of the Entrepreneur: A Journey Of Riches, Book Fourteen
https://www.amazon.com/dp/B07KNHYR8V

Discovering Love and Gratitude: A Journey Of Riches, Book Thirteen
https://www.amazon.com/dp/B07H23Q6D1

Transformational Change: A Journey Of Riches, Book Twelve
https://www.amazon.com/dp/B07FYHMQRS

Finding Inspiration: A Journey Of Riches, Book Eleven
https://www.amazon.com/dp/B07F1LS1ZW

Building your Life from Rock Bottom: A Journey Of Riches, Book Ten
https://www.amazon.com/dp/B07CZK155Z

Transformation Calling: A Journey Of Riches, Book Nine
https://www.amazon.com/dp/B07BWQY9FB

Letting Go and Embracing the New: A Journey Of Riches, Book Eight
https://www.amazon.com/dp/B079ZKT2C2

Making Empowering Choices: A Journey Of Riches, Book Seven
https://www.amazon.com/Making-Empowering-Choices-Journey-Riches-ebook/dp/B078JXMK5V

The Benefit of Challenge: A Journey Of Riches, Book Six
https://www.amazon.com/dp/B0778S2VBD

Personal Changes: A Journey Of Riches, Book Five
https://www.amazon.com/dp/B075WCQM4N

Dealing with Changes in Life: A Journey Of Riches, Book Four
https://www.amazon.com/dp/B0716RDKK7

Making Changes: A Journey Of Riches, Book Three
https://www.amazon.com/dp/B01MYWNI5A

The Gift In Challenge: A Journey Of Riches, Book Two
https://www.amazon.com/dp/B01GBEML4G

From Darkness into the Light: A Journey Of Riches, Book One
https://www.amazon.com/dp/B018QMPHJW

Thank you to all the authors that have shared aspects of their lives in the hope that it will inspire others to live a bigger version of themselves. I heard a great saying from Jim Rohan, "You can't complain and feel grateful at the same time." At any given moment, we have a choice to either feel like a victim of life, or be connected and grateful for it. I hope this book helps you to feel grateful and inspires you to go after your dreams. For more information about contributing to the series, visit http://ajourneyofriches.com/. Furthermore, if you enjoyed reading this book, we would appreciate your review on Amazon to help get our message out to more readers.

Made in the USA
Middletown, DE
02 May 2021